THE FIRST JEWISH SUPERHERO,

From the Creators of *Superman*

By Thomas Andrae

and

Mel Gordon

Preface by

Danny Fingeroth

Feral House

TO JERRY AND JOE

ISBN: 978-1-932595-78-9

10 9 8 7 6 5 4 3 2 1

Feral House
1240 W. Sims Way
Suite 124
Port Townsend, WA 98368

www.FeralHouse.com

Design by Sean Tejaratchi

The creators of SUPERMAN present their NEW HERO:
FUNNYMAN
Trade Mark
by JERRY SIEGEL and JOE SHUSTER
January, 1948
No. 1
10¢

Table of Contents

Danny Fingeroth

Flying Is Easy, Comedy Is Hard vii

Mel Gordon

The *Farblondjet* Superhero and His Cultural Origins 1

Thomas Andrae

The Jewish Superhero 38

Thomas Andrae

***Funnyman*, Jewish Masculinity, and the Decline of the Superhero** 49

Funnyman Comic Book Stories

"The Kute Knockout!" (*Funnyman* #2 March 1948) 86

"The Medieval Mirthquake" (*Funnyman* #4 May 1948) 91

"Leapin' Lena" (*Funnyman* #4 May 1948) 106

"The Peculiar Pacifier!" (*Funnyman* #5 July 1948) 113

***Funnyman* Comic Book Summaries** 121

Funnyman Sunday Strips

"The Many Faces of Piccadilly Pete" (October 31, 1948) 134

"The Tunesmith Caper" (December 5, 1948–January 2, 1949) 136

"June's Makeover" (March 20, 1949) 143

"The Mauler" (April 17, 1949) 144

Summaries of *Funnyman* Dailies and Sunday Stories (1948–49) 145

Funnyman Daily Strips

"Adventures in Hollywood" (Daily Strip: January 13–March 19, 1949) 150

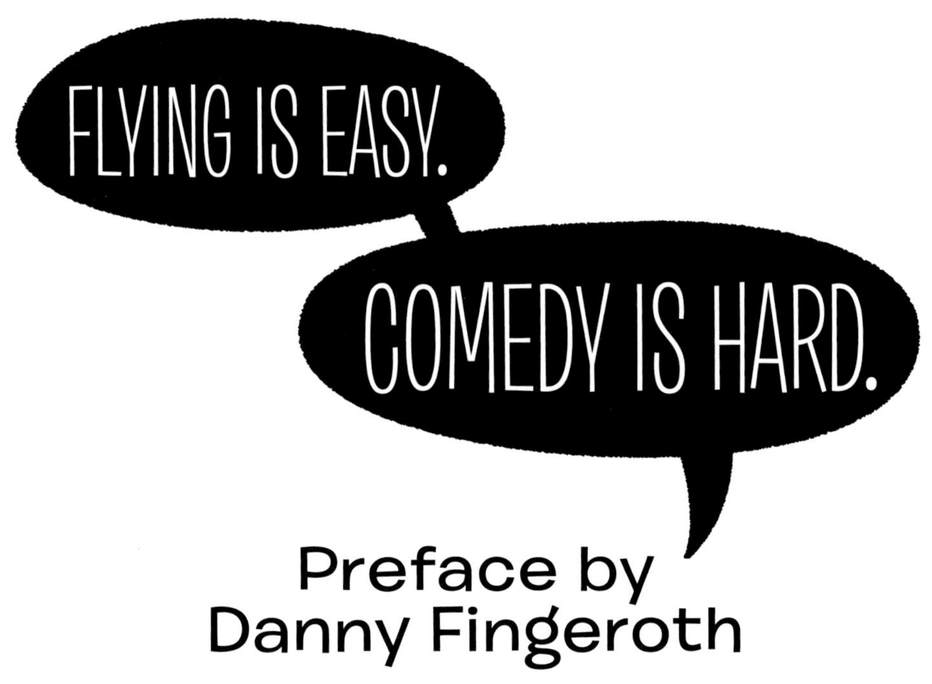

Preface by Danny Fingeroth

Zeitgeist (noun, German): the spirit of the time; general trend of thought or feeling characteristic of a particular period of time.

—Dictionary.com

That zeitgeist is a tricky thing. Most creators never get to grab hold of it, while others have a knack for finding it time and time again. Some have it, lose it, have it again, lose it again. Jolson, Sinatra, Dylan—these are careers with ebb and flow, intersecting with the zeitgeist for a while, then dropping out, then returning. Some get just one really good shot at it.

In comics, Jerry Siegel and Joe Shuster, after years as creative partners, came up with the right hero at the right time:

Superman, the Man of Steel.

Debuting in 1938, Superman defined the zeitgeist of the late '30s and early '40s. Second only to, perhaps, Mickey Mouse, Superman may be the most widely recognized popular culture figure of all time. He embodies a panoply of wishes, dreams, hopes, fears, inspiration, forward-looking anticipation, and backward-gazing nostalgia. It seems like the idea of being so powerful that you can change the world, so compassionate that you only use your great power for good, and so modest that you develop a whole other identity to avoid the spotlight—that is a combination so powerful that it has never gone away, and has been reinterpreted and reinvented over and over. Can all that be chalked up to something as simple as (in the words of Jules Feiffer), "If they only knew..."?

Maybe.

Whatever it was that Siegel and Shuster intuited, somehow this costumed adventurer was the perfect vehicle to express the hopes and anxieties of the late Depression/pre-World War II era, and to express it what turned out the be the perfect medium, the then relatively new form of the "comic book."

Superman + comics books + Siegel & Shuster + National Periodicals Publications somehow ended up equaling something far greater than the sum of its parts. Superman was the hero the world had been waiting for, but didn't know it. The "killer app" of its day. The character was a phenomenon. Any attempt to explain him—like explaining any phenomenon—is retrospective guesswork. After all, if you could figure out how to do it, then people would do it every day. And even the most talented, driven people can't predict what will be a hit and what won't.

Blame it on the zeitgeist.

True, the world was indeed ready for a hero. But the world is always ready for a hero. There are always wrongs to be righted, mistakes to be corrected, flaws to be fixed, villains to be vanquished. Why and how did Superman catch on? Why and how did the character not only ignite the collective imagination, but also spawn an endless stream of other costumed superheroes? What did Siegel and Shuster intuit that no one else did?

There are dozens of theories, and they all have some merit. Many are recounted in this very book, as well as in books by such figures as Peter Coogan, Gerard Jones, and your humble writer. But, really, none of us knows. We can take educated guesses. And we often do. It's a fun and enlightening pursuit. The theories put forth by Thomas Andrae and Mel Gordon in *Funnyman: The First Jewish Superhero*, are among the most interesting of the theories, and uncover fascinating possibilities for the superhero's appeal that I don't think anyone else has explored from quite the same angle.

Whatever the reason, Superman took off, to not coin a phrase, "like a speeding bullet." After him came Batman (who had no superpowers—what was up with that?), The Flash, Green Lantern, Wonder Woman, Sub-Mariner, Captain America. A million of them—figuratively, if not literally. This was the so-called "golden age of comics." Kids, soldiers, everybody was superhero crazy.

Were the superheroes especially "Jewish"? There's certainly a case to be made for the superhero as being specifically Jewish in origin and attitude, but, again, these are retroactive assessments. And at least one Jewish creator of a major superhero denies anything Jewish about that character's creation or content.

One certainly can't deny that many of the earliest and most popular superheroes were created and/or reinvigorated by writers and artists of Eastern European Jewish backgrounds. And human nature being what it is, it seems a safe bet that, try as they might have to not let them—try as they might to have made their stories "all-American" (whatever that means)—their backgrounds were bound to influence that content of their work.

Stereotypes are fascinating and dangerous at the same time. The same can be said for *Funnyman: The First Jewish Superhero*. Andrae and Gordon's thesis is that, while other superheroes may have some earmarks of having been created by young men of Eastern European Jewish roots, Funnyman was more overtly Jewish than any comic book-spawned costumed adventurer that came before.

Now, until seeing this book, you had probably never heard of Funnyman. The character lasted all of six issues in the late 1940s, and for a short time as a syndicated newspaper strip. He was created by the very same Siegel and Shuster who created Superman over a decade before, by the same sensibilities—now more mature and with their craft more refined. Reading Funnyman, one can clearly see it's the work of assured, professional graphic-storytellers (along with their highly competent art studio). The comic took a more lighthearted approach to heroic storytelling than their Superman work, although that material was certainly not without humor.

Funnyman was a comedian who donned a Cyrano-like proboscis and fought zany criminals. Like comedians of the era, including Danny Kaye (whom he resembles), Jerry Lewis, Phil Foster, and Lenny Bruce, Funnyman was a professional comedian. Unlike those comics—who often played mob-run clubs—Funnyman fought crime on the side, using elements of clowning and comedy to overcome his adversaries. In a way, he's a heroic version of Batman's archfoe, the Joker. Clearly, unlike dramatic names like "Superman" and "Batman," Funnyman's code name indicates...well, it's a little ambiguous just what it indicates, isn't it? "Funnyman" is a wink to the reader that the character is an heir to, and simultaneously a satire of, a serious, heroic-fictional tradition. But how is a villain (and hence the reader) to react to an irony-steeped crimefighter in a pre-ironic age?

Still, the concept could have worked. People always like comedians and crime-fighters. Genre satires are perennially popular, too. And if an audience likes a character, they're unlikely to engage in theorizing about its irony or the lack thereof. So a superhero spoof that also satirized a grab bag of popular genres, written and drawn by two talented guys—why didn't it work?

Ya got me.

Maybe he wasn't Jewish enough. Or maybe he was "too Jewish." Read the Funnyman stories reprinted (for the first time in many years) in this volume, and you can decide for yourself. Is Funnyman a schlemiel? A schlimazel? A badkhen? A tummler? A shtarke? A kuneleml? (Don't worry if you don't understand the words. They're Yiddish for a variety of personality types.) In other words, is he a modern version of a cultural archetype? Andrae and Gordon think so—and have the history to back up their theories. Your mileage may differ, but that's the fun of a book like this.

Siegel and Shuster's Superman certainly had a checklist of Jewish and Jewish-y elements: Immigrant. Sent to earth in a Mosaic rocket. Adopted, like Moses was by Pharaoh's daughter. Becomes a fighter against injustice. Pretends to be a nerdy nebbish. (And even if you think of Superman as a Jesus-like savior figure—well...need I remind you of his origins...?)

And then, here comes Funnyman. He looks a little like Danny Kaye. But his humor is forced. There are occasional Yiddish/Jewish references in the stories, but nothing very specifically ethnic. The stories have a crowded, manic look, almost as if they're on the verge of something. But Funnyman doesn't quite get there.

Like Moses, though, he sees the Promised Land.

The ones to get there would be the next generation of not Funnymen, but Madmen.

In Funnyman can be seen glimpses of the outrageous, manic, over-the-top and, quite arguably, immigrant, Jewish sensibilities that would, several years later, make Harvey Kurtzman's *Mad* magazine a huge, ongoing hit, one that would be an influence on modern American comedy, from the underground comics of the 1960s and '70s to *Saturday Night Live* to *The Simpsons* to *The Daily Show*.

Siegel and Shuster fumbled to reconnect with and recapture the zeitgeist, but couldn't grab it again—which was a shame. Because, unlike the situation with their famous lack of participation in most of the riches generated by Superman, they owned Funnyman.

But they didn't own the zeitgeist.

Danny Fingeroth
New York
February 2010

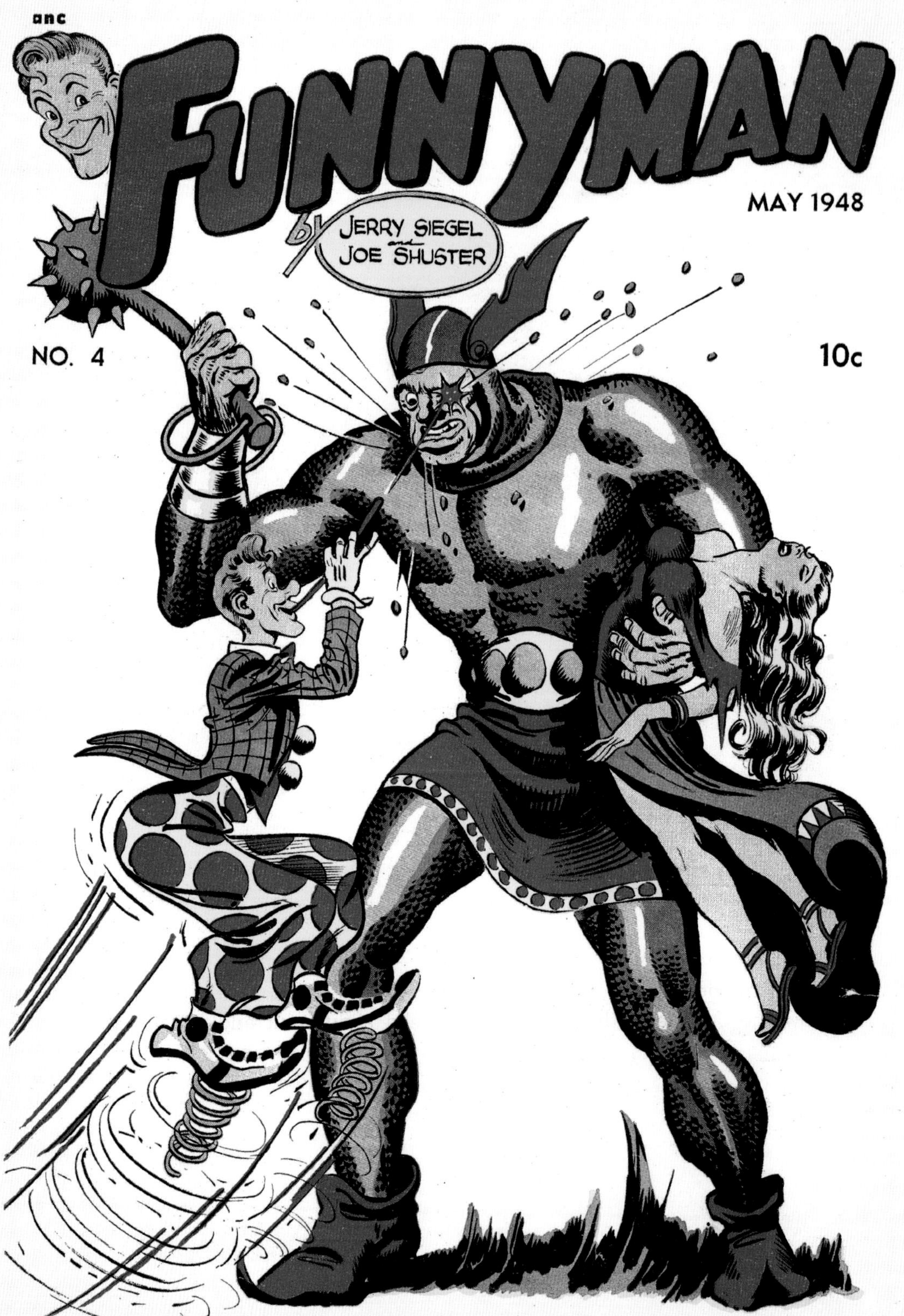

anc
FUNNYMAN
by JERRY SIEGEL and JOE SHUSTER
MAY 1948
NO. 4
10c

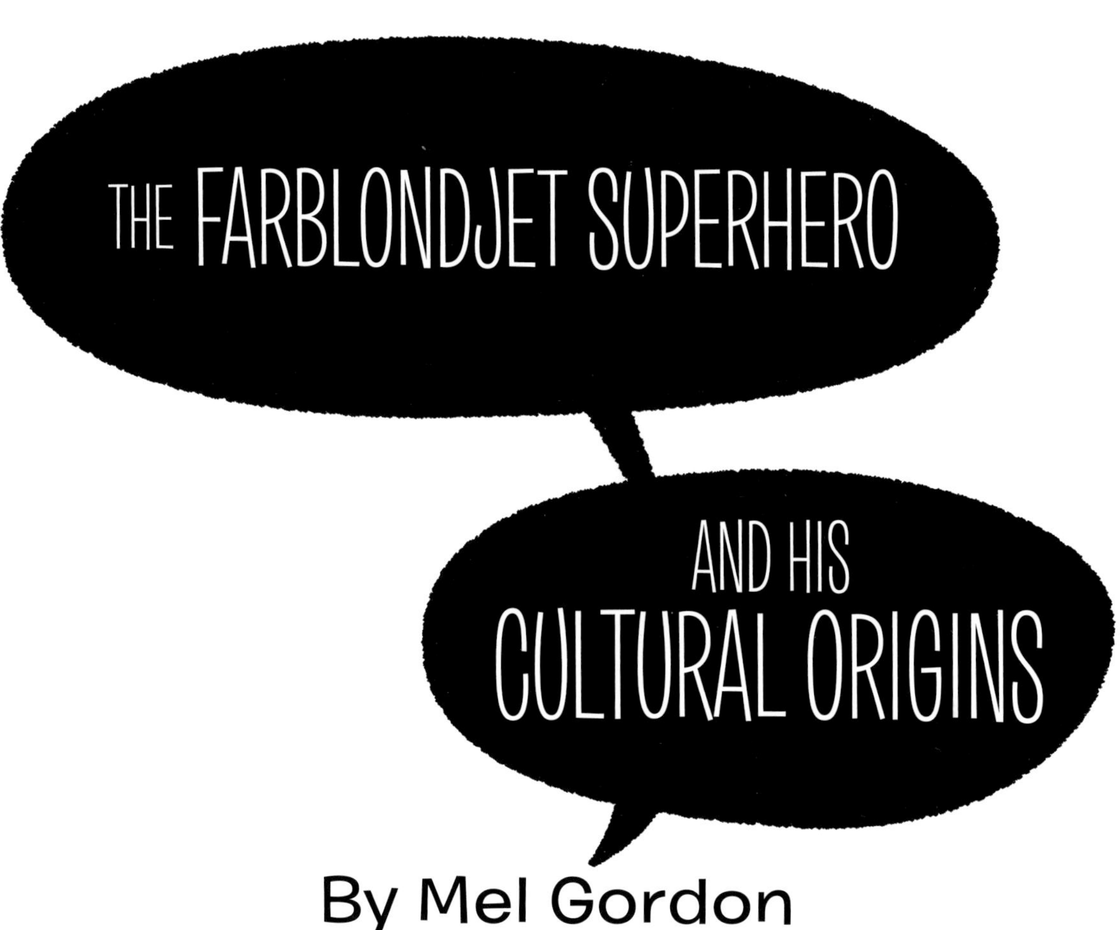

THE FARBLONDJET SUPERHERO AND HIS CULTURAL ORIGINS

By Mel Gordon

In the second week of May 1948, exactly when the Jewish state of Israel was declared and nearly overwhelmed by five invading Arab armies and a dozen indigenous Palestinian militias, the fourth issue of Jerry Siegel and Joe Shuster's *FUNNYMAN* appeared in Bronx corner candy stores and all points west.

It was a time of immense Jewish anxiety. The reassuring wartime images of a beaming FDR and newsreel footage of the Nuremberg Trials were already distant historical salves. Now the Jews and their supporters faced a different and equally determined postwar enemy: the British Home Office, entrenched Arabists and senior officers in the American State Department, discontented anti-New Dealers from the Southern and Rocky Mountain states, a distracted American public, Transjordan's Arab Legion (led by a former British Lieutenant-General), renegade sappers from Britain's Mandate Police Bureau, an underground cadre of SS fugitives (protected by Middle Eastern Vatican envoys), and armed jihadists from Casablanca to Basra.

A down-on-his-luck, jerky (if supremely self-assured) crime-fighter made perfect sense. FUNNYMAN (a.k.a Larry Davis) was an "ace comedian" who thwarted evil and "no-goodniks" through his deadpannery, sneaky sarcasm, clownish athleticism, and glib

Anti-Semitic broadside, distributed by the Christian Nationalist Crusade (Los Angeles, 1947).

rejoinders. He was America's First Jewish Superhero, a carrot-topped Clark Kent who donned a Durante *shnaz* and a seltzer bottle to right the wrongs brought about by thugs, gangsters, and cold-hearted floozies. But this comic-book vigilante was closer in personality and spirit to Siegel and Shuster than their 1938 SUPERMAN popcult colossus.

Larry Davis possessed no superhuman powers, dashing physical attributes, erotic appeal, or capacity to attract a coterie of like-minded citizen crusaders. He could barely cross a thoroughfare unscathed or maintain an even-keeled adult relationship. This feckless action hero did not even own suitable aerodynamic garb.

Funnyman came from no distant constellation—his abode was the Big City streets—and merely relied on his uncanny facilities to deflate, ridicule, provoke, or generate pistol-dropping laughs. Like his creators, Davis' livelihood and means of survival was appallingly tenuous and flimsy: he was *farblondjet*, or practically lost in negotiating his way through the urban-swamp of postwar America. At best, the delusionally upbeat Davis depended on his comic aptitude to befuddle or trip up his adversaries and the world's topsy-turvy recognition of it.

FUNNYMAN
by
JERRY SIEGEL and JOE SHUSTER
HERE HE IS, FOLKS-- FUNNYMAN! A TWO-FISTED HOWLARIOUS SCRAPPER, HE'LL THRILL YOU WITH HIS DARING ATHLETIC PROWESS AND CONVULSE YOU WITH CHUCKLESOME ANTICS! YESSIREE, HE DAZZLES THE LAW TO A FRAZZLE, WHILST MAKING BUFFOONS OUT OF HARDENED CRIMINALS. FOR GRIPPING DRAMA PUNCTUATED WITH GIGGLES AND GUFFAWS, IT'S COMICLAND'S NEWEST AND GREATEST ARRIVAL... FUNNYMAN!
ASTOR
FOUR POSIES
KINSBYS
RKO PALACE
LOEWS STATE
BLANTER PEANUTS

The Mystery of Jewish Humor

Beginning in 1900, Jews have been habitually identified with professional comedy and humor. For many observers, it seemed to be one of their most definable national traits. Even people who have never seen or interacted with individual Jews have routinely acknowledged the connection of Jews with ironic social satire and raunchy parody. For them, the very concept of Hollywood comedy or American television culture conjures up an endless stream of Jewish mass-media gladhanders from Woody Allen, Jack Benny, Milton Berle, Mel Brooks, Lenny Bruce, Sid Caesar, Eddie Cantor, Larry David, Fran Drescher, Danny Kaye, Jerry Lewis, Richard Lewis, the Marx Brothers, Jackie Mason, Gilda Radner, Joan Rivers, Roseanne, Adam Sandler, Jerry Seinfeld, Sarah Silverman, Phil Silvers, Howard Stern, Ben Stiller to Seth Rogen. Yet, before World War I, few academics—outside of Sigmund Freud and his Central European psychoanalytic circles—even broached the subject of Jews and humor.

One Galitzianer to the other: "Vat do you mean I got fleas? Dummy, I'm no dog! Can't you see I got legs?" *Simplizissmus*, 1907.

In fact, throughout the nineteenth century, Jews in Europe and North America were thought to be singularly comic-deficient. Typically, both the noted British and French philosophers Thomas Carlyle and Ernest Renan remarked that Semites in their extensive recorded history lacked any known facility to provoke laughter. In one 1893 British journal, the Chief Rabbi of London, Hermann Adler, maintained that the East European Jewish immigrants setting up shop in the East End were a decent and productive ingathering. His co-religionists, the cleric assured Britain's suspicious readers, were a sternly moral, hard-working, family-oriented, and hygienic people. Hebrews only lacked one fundamental communal asset: a healthy tongue-in-cheek deposition. In a generation or two, he majestically crowed, they would certainly embrace the mirthful folkways of their adopted homeland.

At the turn of the twentieth century, the Jews were commonly perceived to be a humorless, itinerant nation with few acknowledged stageworthy comedians. Just 80 years later, a flipped point of view emerged among cultural historians: the Jews were now considered one of the world's most comic-obsessed ethnic communities and had produced a phenomenal number of professional entertainers on the international scene. In 1978, Samuel Janus, a psychology professor at the University of Pennsylvania, calculated that Jews in America (some 2.5% of the population then) comprised more than 82% of the country's highest-paid comic performers and writers. (And he wasn't including half-Jews, like Bud Abbott, Goldie Hawn, or Freddie Prinze!)

Exactly what happened during the twentieth century to make these wandering Sad Sacks so damned amusing? And whatever historical factors alleviated their gloomy outlook and expressive behaviors, this curious transformation took place everywhere—not just in the show-business oases of North America. Virtually overnight, Jews dominated the humor industries of Berlin, Hamburg, Vienna, Moscow, Warsaw, Budapest, London, Mexico City, and Johannesburg. There had to be some rational explanation. Maybe it could be traced to their peculiar familial mores.

The Construct of Humor in Everyday Jewish Life

Humor is almost always a positive element in normal human discourse. It reduces tension, facilitates bonding, and enhances social cohesion. Joking and wordplay is not just a childish endeavor. It cements and delineates mature relationships. Yet like all collective pleasures, slaphappy antics have set boundaries and limitations. For the Jews, even assimilated Jews or part-Jews, however, humor—especially aggressive humor—can be seen as a shared mania, a construct, a Rorschach of character. A Jew without a facile or quick wit will be inexorably consigned to a lowly slot on the clannish totem.

In the old personnel boxes of giveaway weeklies, *The New York Review of Books*, or in the listings of online dating profiles, Jews are nearly five times more likely to advertise that they have a sense of humor (or are looking for someone with a sense of humor) than Gentile aspirants. More surprising still, among Jewish lesbians, the call for laugh-inducing personality traits in the Women-Seeking-Women columns increases a whapping ninefold.

Frequently, the seeker's Jewish identity is often sunk inside some specialized comic code, like the obvious: "He-brew seeking She-brew." Or with bits of Yiddish: "Let's get *fermisht*! [lost, wacky]"; "Super-slim but *hamisha* [earthy, unpretentious] Gal—That's ME!!"; "*Mensch*-Alert!"; "Playful, green-eyed Buddhist needs outdoorsy, *zaftig* [fulsome] companion." "*Shana madel* [pretty girl] desires same."

***Oy Vey! The Things They Say: A Guide to Jewish Wit* (Riverside, NJ: Andrews McMeel Publishing, 1994).**

For most personal ad-*mavens,* funny is a sexy, vital quality. For self-identified Jews, however, it is the *ekht* [absolute], essential ingredient of a winning, attractive persona. The ability to elicit a geyser of guffaws and/or giggles transforms the *shlub*-like dross of a Woody Allen or Joan Rivers look-alike into beddable or bankable marriage material. (According to the Kenneth Starr Report, one of the first post-oral love offerings that Monica Lewinsky bestowed on Bill Clinton in 1997 was the gift-store hardback *Oy Vey! The Things They Say: A Guide to Jewish Wit.* Even that bouncy, wayward intern never forgot the proper Semitic potlatch: impish sass in the afternoon leads to moans after dark and vice versa. A mere blowjob quickie still mandated some postcoital tribal exchange—in this case, a ten-dollar yukfest of bookish gags.)

Crass humor in the form of wisecracks, teasing, self-referential critiques, and overwrought grievances is still the common currency of daily Jewish life. Forget the manufactured tumult and taboo-piercing rants of Howard Stern. At any suburban Jewish dinner table, doting parents customarily reward their hyperactive kids, no matter how foulmouthed, if they can score a legitimate laugh. Punishment—Montessori or real—is reserved only for the child who attempts vituperative disruption without an apt bite. It is as if the family dullard has failed once again to learn the secret, ancestral language of Hebraic comic invective.

Even torrential outbursts of whining or exaggerated complaining have their station in the panoply of Jewish humor. Unlike their WASP or hyphenated-minority neighbors, Jews often interrupt friends, acquaintances, and business associates in mid-sentence. This dramatically indicates how excited the listener is about conversation at hand and can be interpreted as upright Jewish etiquette. The only occasion when interruption becomes inappropriate is in the midst of a *kvetch* [complaint]. Then the listener is condemned to silence. And the more elaborate and comically primal the *geshry* [outburst], the longer the speaker can justifiably hold the floor.

The Old Theories

In 1916, Freud first recorded the idiosyncratic nature of Jewish humor in *Wit and Its Relationship to the Unconscious*. Jewish jokes were filled ironic puffery, dark gallows illogic, self-mockery, and unnatural amounts of belligerence. The nation that had few contemporary heroes naturally traded in unrelenting sheaves of anti-heroic riffs.

Beginning in 1962, academics explained the unabashed Jewish propensity for insulting humor with three basic theories: the Chosen People mitigated their persecuted status with embittered clownishness, Hebrew culture traditionally incorporated madcap inversions, or, as landless interlopers at the mercy of unsympathetic host countries, Jews naturally developed the disquieting perspective of the uninvited guest.

"Laughter-Through-Tears"

Most Popular Theory: The Jews morphed into a funny people because of their unique diasporic sufferings. Incessant fears of physical annihilation and the day-to-day stress of race-hatred mysteriously transformed the peripatetic Christ-deniers into sarcastic wisenheimers—virtual perpetual-motion comedy machines, *shpritzing* [dispensing] juicy dollops of ironic wisdom. And not only did around-the-clock wisecracking help the lowly Jews maintain their existence in inhospitable climes but their maniacal and self-depreciating retorts utterly confused their hell-bent attackers. What verbal or physical harm can you do to someone who has already denounced himself with such goofy élan?

This is the standard ethnocentric—and tiresome—elucidation, known among scholars as the "Laughter-Through-Tears" theory. Regrettably, it was predicated on one major flaw, history and scientific methodology thoroughly disprove it.

Granted, the "Laughter-Through-Tears" connection is built on two indisputable facts: the Jews endured millennia of oppression in their exile and Jewish entertainers are shockingly over-represented in contemporary comic ventures.

But the "Laughter-Through-Tears" hypothesis doesn't much explain why other persecuted peoples, like the Tibetans, Koreans, American Indians, Armenians, or the virtually forgotten Circassians aren't also internationally known for their biting wit and whimsical patter. In other words, if genocidal torment is the primary catalyst for in-group humor and bitter sarcasm, then there should be at least a couple dozen uproarious Rwandan, Bosnian, and Amazonian Indian standups pacing across our global comic-scape. Nu?

And even in the well-documented saga of Jewish history, the link between suffering and humor is notably weak. The great catastrophes in Jewish life—such as the Destruction of the First and Second Temples, the Crusader cleansing of Europe, the Spanish and Portuguese Inquisitions, the Russian Civil War, to name just a few—produced relatively few celebrated rib-ticklers. Nor is there a recorded incidence where a self-mocking Tevye distracted a narrowly focused Cossack (or a more hip Yiddish-speaking pogromnik) from discharging his sworn duties of looting, raping, or torching a shtetl.

In 1962, Theodor Reik, one of Freud's leading pupils, wrote in *Jewish Wit* that, since the Jews were denied or lacked a sense of the tragic, they emotionally transferred their epic travails into comedy. Behind the Jewish joke was the acknowledgement of doom and "sheer horror." He failed to mention that other isolated minorities in recent history also feared abandonment or extermination. They just didn't joke about it.

"A Laughing People"

The Genesis Theory, of course, goes pretty far back and has an enchantingly simple thesis. It goes something like this: "Hey, the Jews were always funny!" The Genesis adherents maintain that the Jews as a nation were a jovial folk practically before Abraham. Never mind that Egyptian, Assyrian, Greek, and Roman chroniclers forgot to mark this down when they assigned national characteristics to their conquered races. The "Laughing People" hypothesis appeals, naturally, to contemporary rabbinical types, who have assiduously mined chests of Biblical and Talmudic lore for written examples of ironic wordplay and humorous anecdotes.

In the Old Testament, as secularists read it, unfortunately, there is precious little comedy. Biblical heroes like Jacob, Moses, Joshua, Deborah, David, and Solomon, were tricksters, all right. But so were Zeus, Odysseus, Odin, Arjuna, Siddhartha, and Lao-Tzu. Rejoicing at the destruction of one's enemies, while natural and healthy, hardly constitutes the basis of a smart-alecky, sophisticated culture.

Granted, the word "laughter" does appears in the Holy Scriptures but only infrequently and then in the most dreary of circumstances. For instance, in Genesis (Book 2, Chapter 18) Sarah laughs in Abraham's face when her wistful 90-year-old consort informs her that he is about to impregnate her and make her the mother of a sanctified race. Abraham was a good provider and all but, to Sarah, the visionary patriarch had his physical limits. And talk about a tough audience, even God twelve hundred years later complained to Jeremiah that the Israelites were "a stiff-necked people." No, the Bible, by any interpretation, was not a wellspring of tomfoolery.

Traditional Jewish clerical humor veered gently to satirical and polemic themes. Post-Biblical rabbinical comic homilies essentially parodied older forms of prayer and were frequently misogynistic (or occasionally directed against local physicians). A typical literary parody (that has come down to us) is Joseph Zabara's "Prayer for the Henpecked Husband"

(c. 1200). Talmudic writers often indulged in etymological puns and absurdist paeans to wine addiction. But how they really differed from their Christian and Muslim counterparts—except in subject matter—is difficult to assess. True, Jewish communities engaged in raucous celebrations during Purim, the Jewish Spring Saturnalia. But these too closely resembled the local Mardi Gras and Feast of Fools holidays.

If anything in the medieval European ethos, the Jews were associated with exile, epistemological anxiety, implacable misfortune. The ubiquitous image of the Wandering Jew was a study in misery and grotesque torment. A heavy cloud of divine punishment and grief appeared to shadow the Chosen People. Even ecstasy among French Jewish mystics of the early Renaissance was achieved through ritual crying.

"Purim Jesters," ***Sedar Birkur Ha-mazon*** **(Prague, 1741).**

"Outside Observer"

Third Theory: As a permanently marginalized people, the Jews were more attuned to the social hypocrisy that permeated the world around them. After all, as the "schlemiel of nations," the Jews had to grapple, almost daily, with the existential dilemma of being God's Chosen—under His divine protection and so forth—but not witnessing much evidence of it since Daniel negotiated his way out of the lion's den. Therefore, the invisible and heroic underpinnings of all the hierarchical societies where the Jews lived seemed materially suspect to this nation of professional skeptics. Who but the original outcasts could be better positioned to look directly behind the world's hidden inner sanctums and expose them with unerring ridicule?

This theory at least has substance. No other ethnic group has spent so much time and psychic energy debating why its Creator may have stiffed them. Either God is at fault for Jewish deprivation or the Jews themselves are somehow responsible for their

Purim Association Fancy-Dress Ball **Announcement (New York, 1881).**

own maltreatment. Epistemologically, this meant that the ways of Old Testament God were inexplicable (meaning untrue) or the Jews were unworthy of the Divine Covenant (unheroic). This riddle produced the Kabalistic notion of a weak Creator and modern Psychoanalysis.

The Badkhn Theory

What Freud, a century of Jewish social scientists, anti-Semitic ideologues, and innocent cultural bystanders have characterized as Jewish humor—and its exceptionalisms—began in a single day. In 1661, one decade after the conclusion of the Khmelnitsky Rebellion, revered Jewish leaders and rabbis from across the hinterlands of the Ukraine and Poland convened in Vilna. From 1648 to 1651, Cossack bands and Tartars terrorized and devastated the Jewish *shtetlakh* of Slavic Europe. These self-appointed "Elders of the Four Councils" had to explicate why God had withdrawn his heavenly shield from the Chosen Nation.

Most of the Elders believed that the Jews had mimicked far too many volkish practices of their host countries. That was why God did not protect them from the unimaginable horrors that befell the traumatized shtetl survivors. During the Holocaust-like onslaught of the 1600s, whole communities were butchered or dispatched in flames. Worse still, cats were sewn into their wombs of Jewish women after the fetuses had been ripped from their bodies; Torah parchments were shredded and stuffed into the defilers' boots; infants were routinely tossed into nearby wells and rivers.

According to the Council, the 613 Biblical Commandments had to be more strictly interpreted and enforced. In doing so, the rabbis redefined the conventional laws and customs of modern Jewish life. For instance, so many Jewish women had been raped and impregnated by marauding pogromists that the Council decreed that Jewish identity was now determined solely by the mother's racial origin. (Curiously, this contemporary ruling invalidated the Jewishness of nearly half of the kings of ancient Judea.)

The Badkhn, by H. Inger (Warsaw, 1934).

Formalized restrictions on Jewish weddings were also swiftly imposed. Their costs had to be severely curtailed: brides could not wear jewelry or don any finery, the number of celebrants had to be greatly reduced, and customary amusements were vanquished. In fact, extravagant seasonal jollities—even at religious holidays, like Purim and Simkhas Torah—became prohibited.

Before 1648, Yiddish-speaking towns and villages, like the adjacent peasant environs, supported many classes of professional comic entertainers: the most prominent were billed as *Shpilmanern, Letzim, Marshaliks*, and *Payats*. Few nuptial celebrations took place without an assortment of these freewheeling Galahads, inventive master rhymesters, playful showmen, or sleight-of-hand jugglers. Now all of them were strictly banned.

During the July 3rd meeting in 1661, when the Elders formally outlawed the employment of merrymakers, one rabbi inquired about *badkhns* (or *badkhonim)*, the less-than-popular troupes of Jewish insult artists. The Council was temporarily flimflammed. Badkhns were not overtly funny; their usual repartee was personally abusive and generally perceived as unpleasant or rude. To be sure, they could be exempted from the degree.

This clerical decision bizarrely cleaved Jewish entertainment from any Eastern European counterpart and inadvertently stimulated the formation of a unique comic sensibility: hyper-aggressive jousting and obscene effrontery, that is, contemporary Jewish humor.

The word *Badkhn* is of Aramaic origin and first appeared in the Babylonian Talmud, circa 900 A.D. It referred to an imaginary afterlife figure who imitated the worst qualities of

***Badkhn* Postcard (New York, c. 1905).**

unsavory individuals after they passed through death's door. Without a standard concept of a physical Hell among Jewish scholars, this would be a befitting and enduring punishment for all ill-bred rascals and charmless neurotics.

By the late 1500s, the term *Badkhn* was applied to a specific category of Jewish entertainer. For the most part, the Badkhn's nihilistic jabs were directed against the affluent and overly righteous. In one sense, the cynic-in-the-tattered-kaftan was viewed as an anti-Rabbi. He outrageously parodied the elevated lifestyles of the materially comfortable and exalted guardians of the faith. The ragtag and hard-drinking Badkhn had one primary goal: to disrupt or overturn the established social order.

Beginning in 1661, *badkhonish,* by default, became the only known professional comic patter available to the Yiddish speakers of Eastern Europe. We have a reasonably accurate notion of Badkhn routines because so many professional Badkhns engaged in legal deputes over who originated which insulting gags and had the right to repeat them. Rabbinical secretaries transcribed their merciless rants and the rabbis themselves had to determine who could proclaim which cutting slur north or south of Grono.

Badkhns replaced the *Marshaliks* as the MCs at Jewish marriage ceremonies. Before the religious union under the *khupa,* the Badkhn corralled the bride and the bridegroom in isolated compartments and delivered manic lectures about their disappointing and sorrowful futures. It was said that a good Badkhn could make you cry until you nearly went blind from dread and embitterment. At the wedding meal, the Badkhn also sang about the inadequate qualities of the gifts that the couple was about to receive. Typically, the Badkhn would silence the klezmer band that he led during the height of the collective festivity and dispassionately noted that all of the participants, even the youngest, would be worm-infested corpses within 60 years.

At funerals for esteemed shtetl luminaries, Badkhns often interrupted the tearful testimonials with inappropriate table-blessings for the consumption of meat or wine.

Much of the Badkhn humor traded on grotesque eroticism and scatology: homophobic

***Badkhn* Postcard (New York, c. 1905).**

diatribes against limp-wrist *fagelakh* (little birds with broken wings) and fart jokes. Like a champion French pastry chef, who can prepare any number of culinary delights with enough good flour, butter, sugar, and salt, a talented Badkhn could juggle references to drooping breasts, oversized buttocks, small penises, and gaseous excretions into an evening of raucous laughter.

Benjamin Zuskin and Solomon Mikhoels as Badkhonim in the 1925 Moscow State Yiddish Theatre's *Night in the Old Market*.

The institution of the Badkhn flourished for some two hundred years but eventually faded into oblivion as the Industrial Revolution, mass migration, and assimilation upended traditional Jewish life in Europe. Still remnants of the Badkhn's acute satirical riffs and frantic obscenities percolated unimpeded among the Jews fleeing the Czarist Pale of Settlement. It was little wonder that Gentiles thought that nineteenth-century Yiddish-speaking refugees lacked any flair for normative comic interaction.

And the first modern writers and performers in the Yiddish rialto, like the playwright Avrom Goldfaden and the Broder Zingers, were former Badkhns or their descendents. The archaic image of the Badkhn occasionally reemerged on the Yiddish stage as a mocking agent of New World change or foreboding doom. In I.B. Peretz' *Night in the Old Market*, a 1915 mystical spectacle, two Badkhns brought the curtain down with bloodcurdling shrieks and a smug warning against Divine indifference to imminent Jewish annihilation. ("The worse the world, the better our jokes!") *Badkhonish*—in various languages—would follow these immigrant theatregoers into distant climes and form the backbone of their distinctive popular culture.

Characteristics of Modern Jewish Humor

Aggression

All national humors have mean-spirited elements. In most cultures, outward hostility is a minor aspect—around 10%—of the professional or amateur comic material. Among Yiddish speakers, this ratio was wholly reversed. Rarely did Jews take to genteel boasting, lighthearted storytelling, or harmless buffoonery. According to Austro-Hungarian and German observers, Jewish tradesmen on market days engaged in nonstop ludicrous ridicule and noisy physical bouts of one-upmanship. Such alarming behavior was, of course, common among merchants of every ethnicity but the Jews did not seem to be animated by alcohol or the particular business circumstances. Their sneering charades and off-putting hysterical mockery appeared to be unrivaled and possibly inborn.

Even in Jewish delicatessens on the Eastern seaboard, waiters were celebrated for their surly depositions. (Customer: "Are the *kasha varnishkes* [buckwheat groats and pasta] good here?" Impatient Waiter in a deadpan: "Do you see me eating them?")

To be sure, some early twentieth-century Jewish humor did not conform to base Badkhn jocularity. It resembled that of the host country but few immigrant Jews appreciated or subscribed to it.

Sholem Aleichem (Sholem Rabinovich), now acclaimed as the preeminent Yiddish humorist—his Tevye stories were the source of *Fiddler On the Roof*—had only a vestigial Jewish readership during his lifetime. In fact, Aleichem started out as a Russian writer, churning out tender stories about hapless shtetl protagonists. His literary works were inoffensive, comically mild, and indirect, not at all like the inane *shpritery* of his ghetto creations. This may explain why only when Aleichem died in 1916 on Manhattan's Lower East Side did he receive the fame and accolades that he so desired in his lifetime and, decades later, was heralded as Stalin's favorite Yiddish author.

Purim Association Fancy-Dress Ball **Announcement (New York, 1881).**

The Yiddish Language

A derivative of Swabian German, Yiddish incorporated hundreds of Hebrew and Slavic words as Jewish communities relocated eastward, escaping religious fanaticism and forced conversions that erupted during the First Crusade and plague-driven pogroms and expulsions three hundred years later. Yiddish was written in Hebraic script and developed as an independent folk language, or jargon. It generated a rich arsenal of idiomatic expressions and linguistic peculiarities. By 1800, two million Jews used Yiddish as their primary means of communication.

During the period of the Great Migration (1880-1910), many Gentiles heard Yiddish for the first time and were intrigued with its harsh rat–a–tat delivery and odd inflections. For Anglo-Saxons, the vocabulary of Yiddish speakers—even more than their German and Dutch fellow newcomers—sounded funny in the extreme. There were the frequently-heard tangle of words that began with *sh* (or funnier still with *shm*): *shagez* (non-Jewish man), *shiksa* (non-Jewish girl), *shlamazel* (unfortunate soul), *shlemiel* (nonentity), *shlep* (to drag),

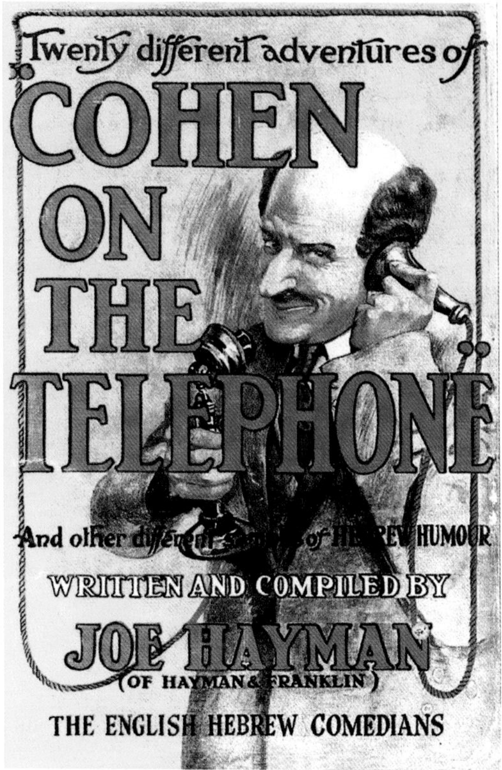

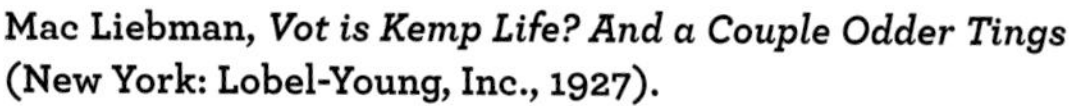

Mac Liebman, *Vot is Kemp Life? And a Couple Odder Tings* (New York: Lobel-Young, Inc., 1927).

***Cohen on the Telephone* by Joe Hayman (New York: George Sully & Company, 1927).**

shlong (penis), *shlub* (physically unattractive type or yokel), *shlump* (to sink), *shmata* (rag or unfashionable article of clothing), *shmeer* (to smear), *shmegagee* (annoying person), *shmekhel* (small penis), *shmendrik* (greenhorn or unwashed dupe), *shmo* (imbecile), *shmooz* (idle chatter or to talk someone up), *shmuck* (penis or inconsiderate person), *shnaz* (nose), *shnook* (patsy), *shnorer* (moocher or beggar), *shpilkees* (pins or agitation), *shpritz* (to spit or joke), *shtik* (private routine), *shtup* (to push or fuck), *shvantz* (snake or penis again), and *shvartzeh* (black person).

Add to those amusing phonemes the Central European difficulty articulating the English *W* or *Ya* and you have one of earliest Jewish-American dialect jokes from the 1880s: a decrepit Jewish peddler ambles around the streets of Atlanta, vainly trying to unload his wares. A line of curious children follows in his path. Finally, the frustrated vender drops his bag of goods, twirls around, and berates the youngsters: "Va's vrong vit you *shlamazels*? Ain't you never zeen a flash-in-blut Yonkee bevor?"

Although Eastern European Jews were commonly perceived as weaklings and easy prey, their language contained almost twice as many words for hitting, striking, and punching human flesh—27—than English. (This was one explanation why Jewish boxing fans routinely tuned in to Yiddish radio broadcasts during the Depression.) Also, Yiddish contained the most abusive words—after Rumanian—of any European language.

This would explain why Jews from non-Yiddish-speaking backgrounds—Sephardic or Mizrakhic countries—were rarely associated with humor, despite their parallel ethnic status and humble origins.

Self-Mockery

This aspect of Jewish humor transfixed both the Freudians and anti-Semites of central Europe. No other ethnic group paraded their shortcomings as readily and as engagingly as the Jews. The most typical archetypal figures in Jewish jokes—Cohen, Goldbaum, Moses—were presented as unappreciative paupers, gaudy *arrivistes*, smug confidence men, shifty merchants, cowardly conscripts, imbecilic flacks, vain matrons, or out-and-out crooks.

Even before the implementation of Hitler's Third Reich in the spring of 1933, Nazi ideologues attempted to explicate and condemn the Jewish propensity for nonstop mockery and invective self-parody. In the pro-Hitler satirical political weekly of 1931, *Die Zeitlupe*, most of the Germanic humor fell flatly on the page. One feature column, however, appeared repeatedly: "Zion Looks in the Mirror." It was an account of Berlin Jewish jokes told by the Jews themselves. Characteristic gag: "Markus Löwenberg is lying on his deathbed. His final request to his wife, Rosalie, is for her to don a revealing lilac dress. Rosalie can't comprehend the dying man's plea. That's her flashy wardrobe for the Jewish Sabbath. Markus insists that she change outfits. After Rosalie returns to his room all dolled up, again she questions her husband's last wish. Markus sits up and explains that when the Grim Reaper appears, who will he rationally choose—a pathetic, shriveled-up tailor or a busty old broad?"

Siegfried Kadner went much further. In his ever-popular treatise *Race and Humor* (Munich: J. Lehmanns Verlag, 1930), which was reprinted in expanded versions in 1936 and 1939, he ranked various ethnic groups according to their sense of volkish humor and professional comedy. Unsurprisingly, the Germans came out as the comic superstars of the civilized world and the Jews the most inferior. (Scandinavians and British placed pretty high; the French and Italian were either too sex-addled or childish to trade in artful hilarity; barely literate American blacks possessed the most animalistic features of the drunken Mediterraneans; sadly, Berlin and Viennese wit was mortally contaminated with toxic doses of detrimental Jewish irony.)

Genuine Nordic jokes emphasized common sense, hard work, virtuous deeds, and social cohesion. Semitic humor was invariably twisted, cruel, bitterly derisive, and solipsistic. The Chosen Nation even mocked their Creator and Protector. In shtetl chapbooks, they presented a beady-eyed Moses on Mount Sinai staring skeptically at heaven: "Let me get this straight! We cut off the tips of our dicks and You promise to take care of us until the end of time! You better put that in writing!"

In fact, the Jews cynically upended any criticism of their race by parading their own criminalities and weaknesses as laugh-out-loud sendups. It was virtually impossible for anti-Semites to scorn nasty *Ostjuden* folkways or futile Judaic endeavors to assimilate into high society better than the Jews themselves. That accursed people had a monopoly on self-deprecation, topsy-turvy storytelling, indelicate hi-jinks, aggressive wordplay, illogic, and obscene denigration. Sure, Berliners adored Jewish comedians; their routines never followed the dictates of superior Aryan merrymaking. And some Jewish MCs delivered German jokes even better than sketch artists born to the Master Race. That was anthropological proof of their ancestral perfidy.

Another tendentious analysis of Jewish humor appeared in J. Keller's and Hanns Andersen's *The Jew as Criminal* (Berlin and Leipzig: Nibelungen-Verlag, 1937). Here, Julius Streicher, the Reich's most flagrant anti-Semite and publisher of the notorious weekly hate-sheet, *Der Stürmer*, introduced and endorsed Kelly and Andersen's quasi-sociological examination of Jewish criminality. Semites, in their objective, Aryan assessment, were genetically predisposed to engage in vile and illicit activities. Moreover, all Jewish culture was poisonously tainted with injurious racial menace and unlawful deceit.

Bizarrely, Keller and Andersen conflated Jewish drollness and joking with lethal anti-German brutality. After surveying the history of Jewish political deception, the Israelite predilection to petty crime, illegal gambling, white slavery, sexual molestation, and pornography, the Nazi criminologists began their chapter on Jewish murderers with a breakdown of Jewish humor. Their self-deprecating repartee and the ability to evoke laughter was one of the Jews' most effective weapons because it obscured and camouflaged their most evil intentions and made them appear to be physically harmless.

***Die Zeitlupe* (Berlin), March 21, 1931.**

"The image of the Jew propagated in the Jewish joke—one of a bow-legged, haggling pest, peddler or shopkeeper—has become one of the greatest successes of the Jewish Nation. It is difficult not to laugh at Jewish jokes. Laughter ameliorates hate and fear, and disdain cripples the will to fight. Their ultimate goal is therefore achieved. The Jew as an outlandish character and petty thief conceals his most destructive quality: his avarice for economic, political and cultural power in the host nation and the subordination of its people under the thumb and the interests of international Jewry. The Jew is not a ridiculous, but a dangerous, creature.

"That image of the hook-nosed, wildly gesticulating, toady,

untrustworthy, and dishonest Jew is even accepted by many opponents of Jewry. They do not doubt that the Jew can accomplish any swindle, any fraud, any trick, but they deny him the aptitude for physical violence. The response to the question: 'Do Jewish hooligans or even murderers exist?' is almost always: 'No!' The reality is something quite different: the Jew is capable of any act, if his own interests or those of his race are served."

For Germans living in the expanding Reich, especially those far from Berlin, Jewish humor was unveiled as yet another tool in the Jews' unending quest for world domination. These were a clever and duplicitous folk. They could even steal an anti-Semitic appellative like "kike" or "heeb" and transform it into a self-mocking honorific.

***Jewish, All Too Jewish: The Chosen People Reflected in Satire* by Wieland der Schmied (Stuttgart: Drei Eichen Verlag, 1934).**

Inversion and Skepticism

Theodor Reik believed that the specific Jewish historical circumstances and disappointment that produced their mania for anti-heroic and inverted humor. After all, the Jewish holy books promised glory and protection; reality revealed something else entirely. Even their God shared their human distress. A devout Jewish worshipper complains that despite his many good deeds and piety, his son is still marrying a *shiksa*. God counters, "You think you got troubles, Horowitz? Look at My Son!"

Traditional Jewish comics deflated both their Almighty and his earthly minions. The Hebrew clergy were portrayed either as dispensers of nonsense—the Wiseman of Chelm—or as natural-born tricksters. Wiley Rabbi joke: A priest, reverend, and rabbi

"Dammit, it's hard to be a Jew these days! The God of Our Fathers dumped Abraham, Isaac, and Jacob in front of this plow and laughed. I just want to write newspaper editorials. Better try my little hand in France." ***Kikeriki*** **(Vienna) April 16, 1933.**

discover a chest of gold coins buried in a cemetery. The priest inscribes a circle in the hollowed grounds. He throws the gold pieces into the air. All the money that lands within the circle will be delivered to the bishop's coffers; the priest will pocket the outlying coins for his own personal use. The reverend draws a line in the soil. The coins that fall on his side will remain with him; the other half will be donated to his church mission. The rabbi then tosses his coins in the air. "Whatever God wants, He'll take."

Scatology

Nostalgia-infused baby boomers have long celebrated Borscht Belt comedy for its unbridled blue or racy material. Scatological and urological setups, female lust, uncontrolled farting, impotency, queer-baiting, and corporally mismatched lovers were its adults-only stock-in-trade. During the 1950s, any hotel guest at Grossinger's could marvel at Pearl Williams' transgressive greeting to a front-row spectator at her midnight show: "What's wrong, honey? I see you're sniffing your fingers. Did you just pick your ass? Oh dear, it was his *takhus* ("derrière")! I hope he showered good. From you people, I get such a *khlop* ("hit," inspiration)!"

To the surprise of resolute bloggers, this kind of public foul-mouthery did not begin in the Catskill Mountains. Badkhns had been perfecting scornful insults and risqué storytelling since Khmelnitsky. Common Badkhn anecdote: That one-eyed Hirsh from Bielsk and his wife were walking down a country lane when Hirsch stopped dead in his tracks to admire a white stallion mounting a mare. "Oy," Hirsch exclaimed, shaking his head, "if I only had another inch more, I'd be a king!" To which his wife countered, "Hirsch, if you only had another inch less, you'd be a queen!"

Jewish mastery of several languages for household and commercial interactions also increased their ability to indecently offend. An innocuous term in one tongue—like *kak* (Russian for how)—could be quickly transformed into a mild obscenity: *kaka* (Yiddish for shit). In fact, many common Yiddish phrases already sounded like bizarre cusswords to

Jewish New Year's Greeting Postcard by Samuel Goldring (New York, c. 1905).

English-speakers: *Mayn pishke is puste!* ("My alms box is empty!") Borscht Belt comedians, of course, had a field day with this. Everyday discourse in one language could garner malicious horselaughs in the minds of others.

***The Battle of the Wits, or Comic Anecdotes* (Budapest: Mordechai Afrim Verlag, 1869).**

Gallows Humor

The certainty of death and all the absurd attempts to sidestep it appears in most national humors but, among the Jews, it incorporated an antinomian and *shlemiel-*

S. Felix Mendelsohn, *The Jew Laughs* (Chicago: L.M. Stein Publisher,1935).

like logic. "You know, Pinkus, if there isn't life after death, I'll laugh."

Shame and irrational desperation always superseded the bleak fate of cartoonish Jewish victims: two *shlamazels* are hauled out before an impatient firing squad. They are offered blindfolds but one of them defiantly refuses it. The first Jew is baffled and nudges his comrade with a shoulder-brush, "Goldbaum, take the blindfold already. And stop being such a *kokhlefl* ["pot stirrer" or troublemaker]!"

Solipsism and Materialism

Self-centeredness and ethnocentric puffery somehow fueled the yuks for much Jewish banter. Freud's favorite Jewish joke: "A Count implores the village Jewish doctor to administer some relief to his wife, who is undergoing a painful delivery. When Cohen enters the castle, he hears the pregnant woman moaning, 'Ach, du Lieber!' The frightened Count asks what the physician can do to comfort the woman. Cohen assures the Count that there is nothing to worry about and asks if he has any playing cards. The two men sit for a friendly game of clablasch. In the next room, the woman suddenly groans, 'Mon Dieu! Mon Dieu!' The Count becomes increasingly alarmed and asks Cohen if he has sedatives. Cohen shrugs his shoulders and suggests a glass of brandy would go well with the game. Finally, the Countess shrieks, 'Oy vey!' and Cohen jumps up from the table. 'Count, it's time!'"

A similar story has the leaders of the world Communism meeting at an international conference in Tokyo. They can't decide in which language to conduct their covert symposium. Russian, after all, is the tongue of the Workers' Motherland; Karl Marx, their esteemed founder, wrote in German; China has the largest number of devoted proletarians; and the host country is Japan. Finally, one of the organizers solves the linguistic conundrum with a wave of his hand. "Who are we kidding? We all know one language! *Red Yidish*! ("Speak Yiddish!")"

Lenny Bruce cleaved the entire world of popular culture into Jewish and Gentile domains, "All Drake's cakes are goyish. Instant potatoes are goyish; TV dinners are goyish. Fruit salad is Jewish. Black cherry soda's very Jewish. Macaroons are very, very Jewish! Lime jello is goyish. Lime soda is very goyish. Titties are Jewish. Trailer parks are so goyish that Jews won't even go near them. Chicks that iron your shirt for you are goyish. Body and fender men are goyish. Cat boxes are goyish. Ray Charles is Jewish. Al Jolson is Jewish. Eddie Cantor's goyish. Evaporated milk is goyish even if the Jews invented it. Chocolate is Jewish and fudge is goyish."

Anna Sequoia, *The Official J.A.P. Handbook* (New York: Plume, 1982).

The Jewish American Princesses jokes from the 1960s also played into the enduring stereotype of the Jewish self-centered and materialist POV but in a pronounced anti-feminist frame. JAPs were targeted as the most spoiled, most shopping-obsessed, selfish, vain, and sexually disinterested of American femmes. (i.e., Q: What do you get when you cross a JAP with a prostitute? A: Someone who sucks credit cards. Or, a definition of Jewish foreplay, two hours of begging.) An early version of the JAP joke appeared in the Twenties. When a hospital physician asks the Jewish night nurse about his deathly ill patient's condition, most of her reply is about how his moaning and requests kept her up all night, ruining her beauty rest. Finally, the dying man stopped pestering her altogether. All in all, it turned into a pretty good night.

American-Jewish Comedy Before 1947

Although German and Sephardic Jews had settled in America long before the Revolution, popular curiosity about these non-Christian immigrants and their strange customs only surfaced in the late 1870s and early 1880s, at the beginning of the mass Jewish exodus from Austro-Hungary and Russia. Lew Wallace's sensationalist novel *Ben-Hur: A Tale of the Christ* (1880), which deflected the story of Jesus and his Disciples onto a fictional Judean nobleman and his phenomenal struggle against Roman-era iniquities and eventual Christian redemption, enormously piqued the interests of middle-class Americans about the stateless, shabbily-dressed newcomers.

George Cooper, *Cooper's Yankee, Hebrew, and Italian Dialect Readings and Recitations* (New York: Wehman Bros, 1903).

Up and down the vaudeville stages of the Eastern seaboard, a craze for Hebe comics erupted. In a rusty plug hat, unfashionable black overcoat, and pointed beard, Frank Bush paced the floorboards, shouting, "My name is Solomon Moses. I'm a bully Sheeny man, I always treat my customers the very best what I can!" His disjointed gesticulations, shameless proclamations, nearly unintelligible English, and ridiculous Hopi-like circle-dance were soon imitated by Burt and Leon, Sam Curtis, Joe Frisco, and Howard & Thompson.

The New York audiences adored these grotesque, addled stage Jews. They mangled the King's tongue and violated all the social conventions of mercantile respectability. It was a new theatrical sensation and a vision of unparalleled mayhem. But none of the top-hatted, bespectacled, featured impersonators were actually of the Hebrew persuasion.

Weber and Fields

The first legitimate Jewish comics in American show business were Joe Weber [*Moisha Weber*] and Lew Fields [*Moisha Schanfield*]. Polish-born, the two adolescent Moishas met up on the Lower East Side in 1876 when immigrant New York was more schnitzel than schmaltz-herring, more working-class Teutonic than Slavic or Jewish. Even among Yiddish-speaking Jews, like Fields' tailor father, German was the common patois of the street and family in the 1870s.

In the dozens of back-alley saloons, honky-tonks, and dime museums below 14th Street, the boys imitated grown-up comic-song-and-dance routines. By the early 1880s, the teenage duo renamed themselves the mellifluous and WASPy sounding "Weber and Fields." They began as a blackface team but quickly moved on to pugnacious Irish types and finally settling into a celebrated eccentric Dutch act of Mike and Meyer (or, at one time, Krautknuckle and Bungstarter).

A growing staple of the New York vaudeville stage, "Dutch Delineators" blended inverted Dutch dialect rhythms with stereotypical German (Deutsch) befuddlement and professorial pomposity. Dutch humor then consisted of imbecilic monologues delivered in a guttural ricochet of "Limburger English." Ridiculous linguistic and visual parody offended neither the Bowery Germans nor native Dutch descendants. What Weber and Fields added to this innocent immigrant pastime was a sharper and more enduring vision of scheming, (not yet American) con-men, boisterous slapstick, insulting patter, and the *luftmensch* psychology of ghetto survival.

Weber and Fields Pictorial Souvenir **(New York: R.H. Russell Publisher, 1901).**

The very sight of Weber and Fields produced shrieks of laughter and immediate applause. Lanky and tall, Fields' Meyer resembled nothing so much as a smooth, big-city Uncle Sam on the make. His dopey, greenhorn victim,

"Weber and Fields" by Al Frueh, *New York World Magazine* (1913).

Mike, played by Weber in a goatee, was padded to look unusually squat and small. Their contrasting sizes and styles allowed for endless misunderstandings and comical bouts. Designed to move more like two-dimensional newspaper cartoons than humans, their aggressive Jewish personas were well concealed inside checkered Dutch-style suits.

Weber and Fields' sketches always revolved around some preposterous—but never successful—con job initiated by the ebullient Meyer on his sweetly stupid *shlub* partner. Typical routines involved a failed hypnotic session with ever increasing repugnant demands and misunderstandings; an invitation to a pool game that unexpectedly cascades into a messy brawl; a phony poker game with newly invented rules to frustrate Mike's good luck; a flight in an air balloon; the purchase of a broken-down hotel; the discovery of a violin.

The breakthrough comic appeal of Weber and Fields was predicated on their violent physicality and disquieting bonds. The couple's slapstick denouements introduced eye-gouging, custard pie tosses, chest-poking, and reflexive shin-kicking to the American public. But unlike more typical "nut" vaudeville numbers, Weber and Fields' antagonistic relationship unveiled all of the elements and dysfunctional logic of a bickering immigrant couple. Even when Mike got choked, pummeled, and beaten, he professed his love to Myer. Spectators roared when Meyer leaped up on Mike's cushioned stomach and poked him deep in his eyes or planted a hatchet in Mike's thick skull (under his wig was a cork-covered steel plate) or broke a violin (or cue stick) over his head. Funnier still was Meyer's justification and Mike's response:

Meyer: "If I'm cruel to you, Mike, it's because I love you." (As he gouges Mike's eyes.)
Mike: "If you luffed me any more, I couldn't stand it!"

By the early 1890s, Weber and Fields became New York's hottest comedy team/anti-team and in 1896 opened their own Broadway Music Hall near Sheridan Square. Their burlesques of popular musicals and melodramas practically obliterated the dramatic originals. The question of Weber and Fields' Jewishness was cleverly deflected by the employment of overtly comic stage Jews like Sam Bernard in their productions. (A tactic Jack Benny would exploit for his radio programs during the Thirties and Forties.)

L. and M. Ottenheimer, One Thousand Laughs From Vaudeville (Baltimore: L & M Ottenheimer Publishers, 1913).

After the turn of the century, Weber and Fields' partnership folded, re-established itself, and folded yet again. Beginning in 1925, they appeared in motion pictures and finally relocated to Hollywood in 1930. Although Fields' children went on to establish a Hollywood-Broadway dynasty, their pioneering ghetto shtik inspired the raucous antics of countless Jewish comedy teams like the Howard Brothers, Smith and Dale, the Marx Brothers, the Ritz Brothers, the Happiness Boys, the Hudson Brothers, and the Three Stooges. (Even the half-Jewish team of Abbott and Costello borrowed several sketches from the Weber and Field repertoire.)

On the Boards

In 1900, Tony Pastor, America's first vaudeville impresario, added authentic Hebe acts to his five-a-day program lineup. A melancholic violin solo introduced the shuffling entrance of the misery-enveloped Joe Welch. This mirthless stumblebum sighed audibly and began his long litany of the day's misfortunes. He always opened with the same rib-tickling, accented refrain, "Mebbe you tink I am a happy man?" His brother, Ben Welch, played an opposite Semitic type, the grinningly optimistic, pushcart salesman. Together,

Will Harris and Harry L. Robinson, "Yonkle, the Cow-Boy Jew" Songsheet (New York, 1907).

they brought down the house and elevated Hebrew monologists to the very top of the comic bill. (Sadly, the Welches' prominence was short-lived: Joe was institutionalized after three years and Ben permanently lost his sight in the middle of a knockabout routine.)

Dozens of Jewish teams quickly followed. Each had its own specialized *shtiklakh* and fan base. Gus and Jay Goldstein marveled at Mendel's ascension to corner cop on the Lower East Side. Monroe Silver complained about the malevolence of newfangled inventions and spiteful telephone operators. Willie and Eugene Howard jettisoned the whiskers and ratty waistcoats to lampoon the desperate charades and foibles of first-generation assimilated Jews on the make.

An accountant at the Philadelphia Telephone and Telegraph Company, Julian Rose often amused his co-workers with lunchtime renditions of a fast-talking Jewish peddler. The laughs began as soon as Rose donned a greasy, black gabardine and pulled an equally rumpled derby hat hard over his ears. Gesturing wildly as he pranced through the office, Rose blathered on in the misplaced rhythms and broken English of the archetypal immigrant Jew. Yet Rose's greenhorn creation varied enough from the whiny vaudeville type to be seen as a comic original. More animated interpreter than Old World crank, Rose's character explained in song the pathetic Hebrew attempts to mimic the rites and mores of the privileged Yankee world encircling him.

Convinced that his true calling was show business, Rose left the 8-to-5 grind at age thirty for the peripatetic life of a "Hebrew i mpersonator" on the Keith-Albee vaudeville circuit. He scored big in the Midwest and Western wheel and was among the first Jewish comedians to record on Edison cylinders in 1903. Rose's peculiar, superannuated dialect parodies—his Yiddish-inflected patter was once clocked at two hundred words per minute—served him well in the recording studio, where his recordings achieved a strong Jewish and Gentile following. "Sadie's Birthday Party," "Mrs. Blumberg's Boarding House," "Becky, the Spanish Dancer," and "Levinsky's Wedding" formed the basis of Rose's spoken repertoire.

Other Jewish comedians and songwriters imitated him on cylinders and 78 disks with such novelty songs as "When Moses With His Nose Leads the Band," "Under the Matzos Tree--A Ghetto Love Song," "Yonkel, the Cow-Boy Jew," "Marry a Yiddisher Boy," and "Cohen Owes Me $97."

"Eddie Cantor" by Frederick J. Garner (St. Paul, MN: Brown & Bigelow, 1933).

Rose's sudden desire for legitimacy on Broadway in 1905, however, considerably shortened his American career when he starred in *Fast Times in New York,* a comedy that was much criticized for its vulgar portrayal of Jewish life. The ubiquitous image of the disheveled Hebrew comic and his babbling monologue about insurance scams gone awry certainly beguiled small-town vaudeville audiences but respectable Jewish organizations were laughing less. The Chicago Anti-Stage Jew Ridicule Committee, among many, militated against Rose and his unshaven brood. By 1913, Rose found himself blackballed from Keith-Albee bookings altogether, forced to rely on smaller and less lucrative live venues.

Six years later, billing himself as "Our Hebrew Friend," Rose moved permanently to Britain. Within two years, he found himself engaged as a headliner at London's Palladium and was one of the first comics to be heard in BBC broadcasts. At the end of his life, Rose was a featured celebrity in the Royal Variety Performances. In a sense, Julian Rose created the "Jewish nut" character for future British culture, a type that would be revived (without the dialect) in every half-generation from Issy Bonn, Bud Flanagan, Jimmy Gold, Peter Sellers, Marty Feldman, Ben Elton, to Sacha Baron Cohen.

In his annual *Follies,* which reached their apogee during the glitter of the Jazz era, Flo Ziegfeld utterly transformed the image of the razzle-dazzle, Jewish Broadway clown. As New York City's most indefatigable and influential showman, he had already established Anna Held, a former Yiddish theatre chorus girl, as the national avatar of modern sexuality—his publicists maintained that the flapperish, milk-bathing Held was raised in a French convent. During the Great War, Ziegfeld equally advanced the careers of Ed Wynn, Eddie Cantor, and Fanny Brice. They were soon to be heralded as the hip primitives of the Counter-Prohibition.

If Wynn, known as the "Perfect Fool," traded on his pip-squeak pathos and tiny porkpie felt hat, Cantor and Brice cavorted around Ziegfeld's stage in broad Hebraic burlesques of high-stepping Manhattanites. Billed as the "Apostle of Pep," Cantor infused the traditional pabulums of shtetl Jews—cowardice and hypochondria—with vivacious bursts of energy and a delirious sex drive. The mere thought of nestling on a Morris chair with a long-stemmed babe galvanized the Lower East Side standup into beads of eye-rolling and patty-cake emoting pivots.

Cantor studded his vaguely Jewish characters with bits of Yiddish patter that only the initiated might decipher correctly—Cantor-Tailor to a Gentile Client: "You want a *patsh* ("a hit") on the sleeve? I'll give you a *patsh!"* [slaps the customer's face]. Brice, soon to be marqueed as "America's Funny Girl," went all-out ghetto. She crossed her eyes and stooped to emphasize her hooked nose while belting out comic and torch songs in vulgarly inappropriate Yiddish inflections. Ziegfeld's erotic extravaganzas were now bound to Hebe acts in a contemporary mode.

Ziegfeld's revue imitators, Irving Berlin, George White, Earl Carroll, and the Schuberts, also set Jewish comedy sketches between their near-nude music-hall parades. Fresh from the vaudeville and burlesque circuits came Lou Holtz, the Howard Brothers, the Ritz Brothers, Ben Hecht, and Walter Winchell. New York critics waxed rhapsodic over the anti-heroic schemes and comic vanities of these new Stage Jews.

The Borscht Belt

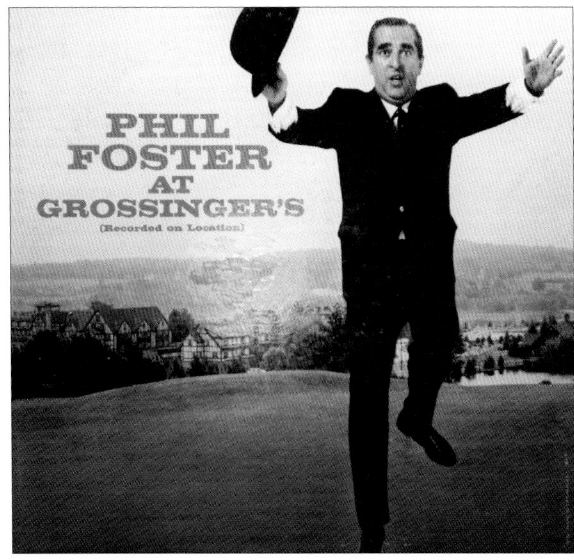

"Phil Foster at Grossinger's" Album Cover, 1957.

In the Catskill resort region, one hour from New York City, working- and middle-class Jews spent much of their summers in rented bungalows and small hotels. (There were 500 hotels and 3,000 bungalow colonies in the area by 1945.) While Irish-Americans and Italian-Americans were content to enjoy their holidays in the natural tranquility of Sullivan County with its endless outdoor and family activities, Jewish vacationers demanded comic amusements as the constant feature of the late-night entertainments.

In the Catskill adult summer camps and lodges, "social directors" or amateur performers, usually waiters, had to confront angry and restless Jewish spectators on inclement days. Because of the comics' ceaseless activities to please that difficult clientele, they became known as "toomlers." Masters of improvisational invective, these early standups recapitulated the social role of their Yiddish-speaking progenitor, the Badkhn. This led to the institution of the Borscht Belt comedian, the filthy-mouth scrapper *par excellence*.

Fanny Brice in "Modernistic Moe," a parody of Martha Graham's solo political-dances, *Ziegfeld Follies of 1936*. Drawn by Al Hirschfeld, *New York Times* (September 15, 1936).

Borscht Belt humor as a definable genre developed in late 1920s and the early 1930s, just when the mainstream Jewish comedians were camouflaging their ethnic origins to perform in the new mass media of radio and sound feature films. Most of the Bronx dwellers and Brooklynites altered their surnames—often pushing their Christian names into last place—and concocted more elegant backstories.

Some playhouses, like the one at Grossinger's (or G's), were professionally-sized and sat 1700 ticket-holders. Slapdash satires of Broadway musicals and Hollywood movies, dirty standup, and biting parodies were the order of the day. Typically, the ten o'clock and midnight shows mocked the hoteliers' mammoth propensities for platters of complimentary kosher food, ill manners, illicit business dealings, and bed-hopping pursuits. (This was a prime watering hole for JAPs seeking young professional mates. Again, laughs led to sexual misbehavior and, if successful, to sumptuous bridal parties.)

By 1942, the toomler as popular entertainer slowly died out because of the wartime draft and changes in tastes among assimilated Jews. Downscale sketch parody—the more ludicrous, the better—was more to their liking. The tradition of gross-out Badkhn-toomler humor, however, resurfaced helter-skelter in the less lavish hotels and among New York nightclub comics in the late Fifties.

One adult game, "Simon Sez," invented by Lou Goldstein at G's, soon became a manic national pastime. What most native Americans never realized were the particular Jewish roots of Goldstein's aggressive contest: following the implicit orders of the authority figure too quickly would soon result in a default (or death by Cossacks).

Both Kutscher's and Grossinger's attempted to excise Jewish comic entertainment altogether in the late Forties for the more All-American diversions like basketball and

Rehearsal photograph of Mickey Katz, Phil Foster, and Joel Grey in the *Borscht Capades of 1951*.

baseball. Unfortunately, a series of college sports scandals involving Jewish bookmakers, point-fixing, and the said resorts occasioned the return of ribald, Badkhn-like comedy until the demise of the Borscht Belt in the 1970s.

By the Fifties, the hostile humor of the Catskills leaked back into Manhattan. Will Jordan and Lenny Bruce were sending shockwaves into New York's premier nightclubs, ripping into the social hypocrisies and sacred cows of the era. Even Gentile standups—especially Italians and African-Americans—suddenly accommodated themselves to this bad-taste frenzy. *Esquire* magazine billed this phenomenon as "the Yiddishization of American Comedy." You didn't even have be Jewish to engage in dirty-mouthed Borscht Belt antics. (The stereotypical tired Catskills raconteur found new life in the 1980s and 1990s with Eddie Murphy's cigar-chomping Gumby; Paul Fusco's Alf, an offensive alien puppet creature; and Robert Smigel's ferociously memorable "Triumph, the Insult Comic Dog.")

The Wasp (San Francisco), June 9, 1888.

Cartoons and Jokebooks

Caricatures of the Jew as a surly imp appeared on the front pages of America's graphic weeklies since the early 1880s. Jewish bodily features—furrowed foreheads, thick eyebrows, baggy eyelids, uneven teeth, hairy double chins, pudgy stomachs, knock-knees—were easy to draw and always produced quick laughs. Whether portrayed as maniacal immigrants or as ersatz Americans, hysteric Hebrews were immediately recognizable. First-generation Italian- or Irish-Americans had to be properly captioned and their dialect conversations were mostly predictable and a bit tiresome. Jews had always something innovative to whine about.

Although comic strips graced the pages of Yiddish dailies since the early Teens, Harry Hershfield created one of the first sympathetic Jewish cartoon characters in the national press. Abie Kabibble, or "Abie the Agent," a car salesman, debuted in 1914 in the *New York Journal* and became syndicated in the Sunday supplements within a decade. Abie's commercial and familial troubles evoked good-natured chuckles across the pop landscape. He was the subject of Tijuana Bibles, dialect songs, silent movie animations, and early

Harry Hershfield's *Abie* (June 22, 1929).

Left: Jo Swerling, Arthur Johnston, and George Holland's "Abie! (Stop Saying Maybe)" Songsheet, 1926. Right: Milt Gross, *Dunt Esk!!* (New York: George H. Doran Company, 1927).

radio. Groucho Marx even referenced him in *Animal Crackers.*

Rube Goldberg, Mac Lieberman, and Milt Gross fashioned their own Hebraic types. By the mid-Twenties, Gross' Mowriss Feitlebaum and his tenement family formed the basis of two best-selling graphic anthologies. Jewish jokebooks and collections of humorous anecdotes were a pre-Depression staple. Even the YMCA's handbook of "skits and stunts," *The Omnibus of Fun,* was penned by the husband-and-wife team of Helen and Larry Eisenberg.

Charlie Chaplin in *The Immigrant*, 1917.

Hollywood Talkies and Syndicated Radio

Although Hollywood's institutional beginnings were heavily Jewish, few silent comic headliners themselves were of the faith. (Charlie Chaplin was the luftmensch stand-in for the hapless immigrant.) The sound revolution in features—inaugurated by Al Jolson in *The Jazz Singer*—brought New York Jewish comics into the mix.

Eddie Cantor, the Howard Brothers, Al Kelly, Fanny Brice, Lou Holtz, the Three Stooges, Jack Benny, the Marx Brothers, George Burns, the Ritz Brothers, Benny Rubin, Milton Berle, and Phil Silvers globalized Jewish revue and burlesque routines.

Over the radio waves in prewar America, it was near impossible to avoid the snap of Yiddishisms and Jewish comic personalities. Cantor disguised his old Ziegfeld routines by playing straight man to Bert Gordon's obviously Jewish "Mad Russian"; Artie Auerbach responded as the fearless *schlemiel*, "Mister Kitzle," to Benny's cheapskate taunting; an

1000 Jokes Magazine #40 (October-December, 1947).

incredulous Berle interrogated Arnold Stang's smugly facile Francis, the most irritating and nasal of all Outer Borough *shnooksters*.

Fred Allen, the Gentile King of network radio, interviewed his own panel of urban misfits, Allen's Alley, that usually started with Mrs. Nussbaum. Played by Minerva Pious, the malapropism-prone Bronx denizen almost always responded with a deadpan rejoinder, like, "You were expecting maybe Veinstein Chuychill?"

But of all of the Jewish comic leads who rode the Borscht Belt to the Hollywood bandwagon during the Depression and war years, none transfixed Jerry Siegel more than Danny Kaye (born David Daniel Kaminsky). Here was a buffoon who shifted from fall-down physical clown to agitated musical maestro to charming juvenile in the beat of a snare of a drum or blink of an eye. He was Funnyman incarnate, a Walter Mitty who could deliver a bully-deflating *shpritz*.

Milton Berle, *Out of My Trunk* (New York: Grayson Publishers, 1945).

THE JEWISH SUPERHERO

By Thomas Andrae

Superman is only the latest in a long line of Jewish heroes with great strength. The biblical Samson was one of the strongmen who inspired Jerry Siegel's creation of Superman, and critics have also suspected that the Golem, a legendary creature of Jewish folklore, was also a major inspiration, although this has not been confirmed—until now. Speaking of the influences that led him to create Superman, Siegel writes: "I recall being very favorably impressed by a movie entitled *The Golem.*" [1] The movie was about an "avenging being" who uses his gigantic strength to "crush a tyrant" and "save those who being were oppressed," Siegel explained. *The Golem: How He Came Into This World* was released in 1920 and is considered a classic of German Expressionist Cinema. It was the last of three golem films directed by Paul Wegener (who also played the golem in the film) and featured Karl Freund, one of Germany's greatest directors, as photographer. German Expressionism

Mikás Ales, *Rabbi Lowe and the Golem* (1945).

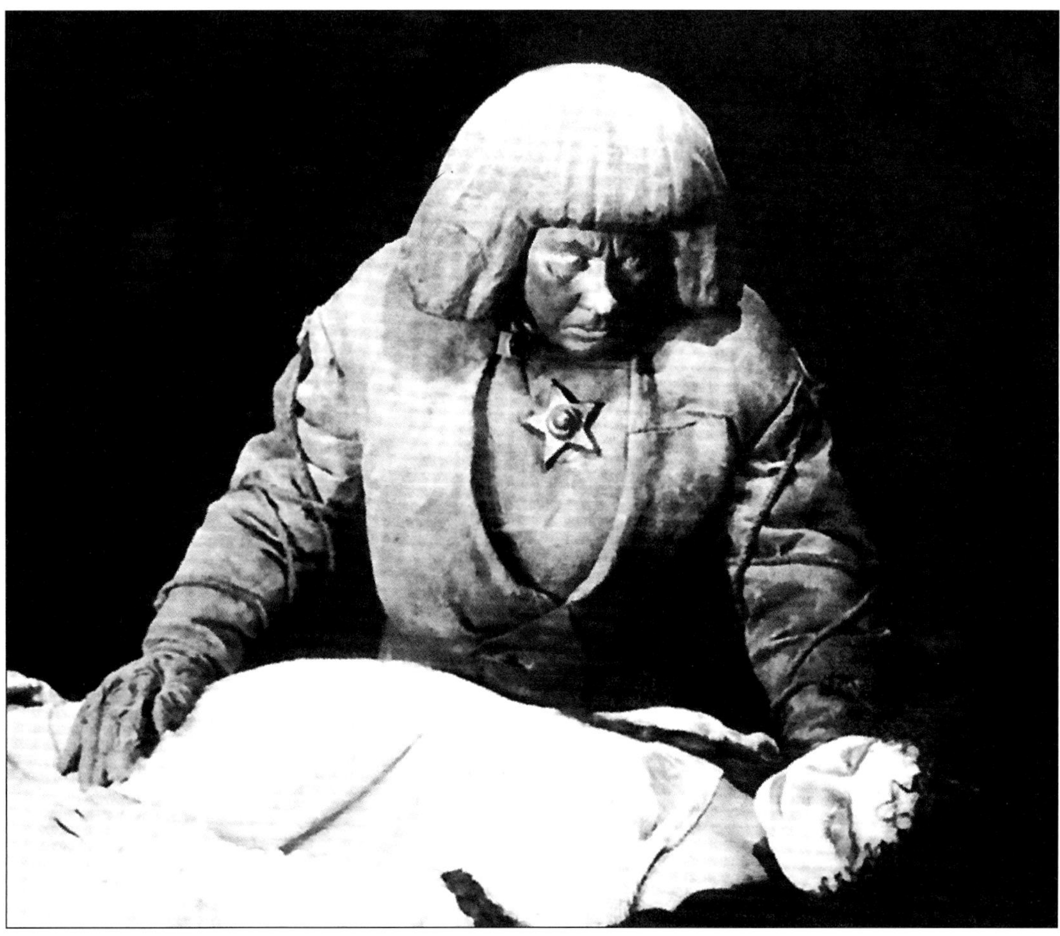

was noted for using lighting, shadows, and special effects to portray psychological and spiritual themes and for making use of cinema's unique ability to visually depict fantasy and magic.

The golem was an ancient Jewish legend about the creation of a gigantic being out of clay. The word appears only once in the Hebrew Bible, in Psalms 139:16, and became part of Jewish folklore during the Middle Ages. The word can be traced to the Hebrew "golem," which means "shapeless matter." In Yiddish it is often used as an affectionate insult meaning "ignorant person" or "dummy" and signifies something imperfect and unformed. The golem is mentioned in the Talmud and a number of early sources but the classic version of the legend is that of Rabbi Loew and the Golem of Prague. It first appeared in print in the 1847 collection of Jewish stories, *Galerie der Sippurim.*

Wegener drew upon this legend for his film. The Golem featured two historical figures: Rabbi Loew and Rudolf II, the Holy Roman Emperor, both of whom lived in the sixteenth century and met on a number of occasions. Lowe was a master of the Jewish mystical teachings in the Kabbalah and known to scholars of Judaism as the Maharal of Prague, or simply The MaHaRaL, the Hebrew acronym of "our teacher, Rabbi Loew." In one story,

he used his knowledge to create a huge creature out of clay to force Rudolf to rescind his order forcing the Jews from Prague, where Rudolf had his capital. Much of the persecution of Jews derived from religious conflicts with Christians. In the film the Christians accuse the Jews of practicing black magic and destroying their religion.

The Golem portrays the Jews' plight sympathetically showing the centuries of persecution and anti-Semitism they have experienced and their longing for a messiah: "Throughout their history," writes historian Arnold Goldsmith, "the Jews of the Diaspora looked for heroic figures who could mitigate their suffering and lead them to the messianic redemption their religion taught them to expect." [2] Thus, the golem may be thought of as the first Jewish superhero prototype, whose gigantic strength could not only protect the Jews from persecution but also bring about the end of their exile.

However, the golem of both legend and film is not a heroic being but an unruly, destructive monster.[3] In Wegener's film, the golem turns on his creator when he tries to take the shem (a paper with the word AMET, the Hebrew word for truth i.e. God) from his chest to de-activate him. Huge in size and threatening to dominate his creator, the golem is a symbol of id-like, repressed emotions. The film's subtext constitutes a warning about their release and that the Jews must not let their anger erupt in irrational violence towards their persecutors. Loew's helper, Famulus, becomes jealous when Loew's flirtatious daughter Miriam begins a seduction with the king's messenger, Florian, and he orders the golem to seize Famulus. The giant throws him from the tower, starting a conflagration in Loew's laboratory, then abducts Miriam who has fainted. The monster escapes into the city, going on a destructive rampage that threatens the entire Jewish ghetto. He is brought down only when a little girl offers him an apple and plays with the Star of David in his chest, which contains the Shem, causing him to become deactivated.

Critics have claimed that Mary Shelley was inspired by the golem legend in her creation of Frankenstein in 1818. The influence can also be discerned in the cinematic adaptations of Shelley's monster. James Whales' 1931 horror classic Frankenstein is strikingly similar to Wegener's film. Frankenstein's laboratory scenes, the monster's aversion to fire and the scientist's burning tower, the monster's built-up shoes and shuffling gait, the scene of a small girl offering the monster a gift (in Frankenstein it is a flower), and the monster's muteness (in Mary Shelley's novel he is quite articulate) all originate in The Golem. Frankenstein also adopted the German Expressionist visual style of Wegener's film. Thus The Golem has had a seminal influence on the legions of monster films that followed in the wake of Frankenstein.

The golem's affinity to the Frankenstein monster makes the Jewish creature an important progenitor of Superman. The Frankenstein monster was the first superman in science fiction literature created by pseudo-scientific means. Following the lead of the Frankenstein monster, the superman in science fiction had had been cast as a deviant and threatening Homo Superior, a being of the same genus as man but physically or mentally superior to normal humans. Although sometimes a sympathetic character, the superman was so dangerous he had to die or be robbed of his power by the end of the story.

Following this tradition, Siegel's first superman story was about a villain, not a hero. "The Reign of the Superman" was the story of a mad scientist's experiment with a downtrodden man from the breadline that transforms him into a mental giant who uses his powers to steal a fortune and to attempt to dominate the world. The story appeared in the January 1933 issue of Siegel's science fiction fanzine, Science Fiction: The Advance Guard of Future Civilization. Drawn by Shuster as a bald-headed, maniacal creature, Siegel's superman was an exact look-a-like of Superman's archenemy, the mad scientist Luthor. Siegel's creation of a heroic superman was an innovative break from science fiction tradition and reconfigured the Jewish longing for a powerful messiah. Superman was not a power-mad tyrant nor alienated from society but a "savior of the helpless and oppressed," who, disguised as Clark Kent, lived among ordinary humans.

Although Superman's Jewish roots were hidden for years they became the subject of a 1998 comic book story. The artist/writer Jon Bogdanove and writer Louise Simonson created a story for Superman's sixtieth anniversary appearing in a three-part serial in the Superman title Man of Steel (#80-82). In this story Superman becomes a golem defending the Jews of the Warsaw ghetto from the Nazis. Two children, Moishe a budding writer and Baruch, a young artist, representing Siegel and Shuster, create stories about an "angel" who "would save us." The celestial being is a caped and costumed figure who looks like Superman. When the Man of Steel actually shows up and aids the Jewish resistance in fighting the Nazis, the German soldiers who flee in terror from him tell their superiors about the fearsome "Golem." For the first time in comics, a direct connection was made between the golem of legend and the Last Son of Krypton. [4]

A real-life Jewish strongman may also have had a formative influence in Superman's genesis. In the winter of 1923 Vienna was experiencing ominous events: bloody confrontations were taking place between monarchists and socialists, and the Nazi Party was involved in violent street confrontations. Yet, for several months these events were almost eclipsed by an event in popular culture. The Viennese public was enthralled "by a phenomenon that has simply never been witnessed," Reported the Wiener Sonn-und Montags-Zeitung:

Illustriertes Weiner Extrablatt, *Modern Sam son* (January 3, 1923).

> *A human being of supernatural powers. Breitbart. He bends steel as if it were soft rubber, bites through chains as though they were tender meat, drives nails into thick wood with his bare fist....A bridge loaded with hundreds of kilograms of concrete block is lowered onto his gigantic body, and the blocks are pounded with hammers....He uses his body as a support for a manned carousel which revolves at dizzying speed.* [5]

All of this, gushed the reporter, "is enough of a sensation to astonish the Viennese. Breitbart, Breitbart, Breitbart. No one talks of anything else. No one else is the subject of so much admiration." [6]

Siegmund Breitbart was a Yiddish-speaking strongman from Poland. The son of a poor blacksmith, "Zishe," as his Yiddish audiences called him, was billed as the "Strongest Man in the World" and the "Iron King." Blending spectacular showmanship and genuine strength, Breitbart became famous in Europe and America. In 2001, *Invincible,* a film directed by Werner Herzog, updated the Breitbart legend to the 1930s in a tale involving him with the clairvoyant and mentalist Erik Jan Hanussen and the Nazis.

Breitbart appeared on stage in costume as various archetypes of masculine heroism: a bullfighter, a cowboy, a gladiator, and a Roman centurion. Breitbart also appeared on stage as Bar Kokhba, who led a revolt against the Roman Empire in 132 A.D., establishing a

From Breitbart promotional booklet on his 1923 North American tour.

Jewish state of Israel, which he ruled for over two years, until the Roman army crushed it. It was the last successful attempt of the Jews to create a homeland until the establishment of the State of Israel in 1948. He was acclaimed as a messiah, a heroic figure who could restore Israel's past.

In a time of rising anti-Semitism, Breitbart did not hesitate to identify himself as a Jew, appearing onstage with a Star of David below his name. Jewish audiences called him Unzer Shimshon hagibor, "Samson our hero." In Vienna, it was reported that pictures of Breitbart adorned numerous Jewish shops and workshops and that in synagogues prayers were offered for his success. Eastern European Jews saw Breitbart's vaudeville acts as invigorating responses to the ever-growing threat of anti-Semitic ideologies and attacks. According to Gary Bart, producer of *Invincible* and a descendant of the Jewish strongman, a popular Yiddish saying was that "were a thousand Breitbarts to arise among the Jews, the Jewish people would cease being persecuted." Breitbart saw himself as a modern Samson who could empower Jews by teaching them self-defense and how to be physically strong as a response to their political powerlessness. A Zionist, he publicly called on Jews to join him in an army that would eventually liberate Palestine, then controlled by Britain.

As Sharon Gillerman notes, Breitbart was able to appeal to Jews and non-Jews alike.[7] He challenged racial categories and undermined stereotypes of the Jew. Jewish audiences in central Europe praised his body for both its beauty and its strength, seeing Breitbart

Cleveland Times,
October 31, 1923.

Vodvil Presents Siegmund Breitbart Superman of Strength

Breitbart, the Iron King, has some new stunts for his second week's program at Keith's. Yesterday afternoon he assayed to bend an iron beam used in construction work, using his neck as the point of contact—but he accomplished this extraordinary feat. He allowed about a dozen men to get on each side of a 32-foot I-beam which was placed on his head, and smilingly permitted the crew to bear down with all their might to bend it on his head. Bending iron bars and snaping chains is like playwork to this Hercules, and his entire act is almost unbelievable until you see it.

With a dozen men on each side, a 32 ft. stee
This requires powerful allround developı

n resting on my head is bent as here shown.
acquired through my system of training.

SIEGMUND
BREITBART

as the embodiment of contemporary ideals of strength and beauty. His blue eyes, light hair, and muscularity led both Germans and Jews alike to claim him as a representative of their race. While Germans commented on his blond hair as a sign of his Aryan beauty, Eastern European Jews pointed to his blonde curls as typical Semitic features. Breitbart's physical perfection thus allowed different audiences to interpret his body in contradictory ways. Breitbart's emphasis on teaching muscle building through correspondence courses undercut racialist theories by showing that acquiring a muscular physique was the result of exercise, not genetics, and could be acquired by everyone.

Breitbart arrived in America on August 26, 1923 and toured widely throughout the United States. Billed as "The Superman of the Ages" in papers across the country, he performed in New York's Hippodrome before more than 85,000 people during Christmas week of 1923 earning $7,000 a week, a princely sum at the time. He appeared in Cleveland, Ohio in October 1923 performing at B. F. Keith's Palace Theater. To advertise his act, Breitbart staged several public stunts, wearing his signature Tarzan costume. In one appearance, the strongman held the traces in his teeth of a harness attached to a 20-foot scenery truck filled with 60 people while two horses pulled it down Lakeside Avenue N.E. from city hall to the new courthouse. Breitbart's performances were noted in all the Cleveland newspapers. The *Cleveland News* (October 11, 1923) announced that "Hercules Could Get Tips From Breitbart." And, the *Cleveland Times* (October 21, 1923) reported that "Vodvil presents Sigmund Breitbart: Superman of Strength."

Breitbart died prematurely in 1925 as a result of a stage accident when he accidentally drove a rusty nail into his leg giving him lead poisoning. But his fame outlasted his death. His Eastern European Jewish fans, who had been responsive to his message of Jewish empowerment, passed on stories about him that are still being circulated today. His correspondence course, which was based in London and New York, kept his name alive and operated years after his death. His cable address was simply: "Superman–New York." Jerry Siegel was nine years old when Breitbart came to Cleveland. Infatuated with strongmen like Samson and Hercules, Siegel may well have seen or read about the Jewish strongman whose nickname was "Superman" and appropriated the name for his new superhero.

Notes

1 Jerry Siegel, *The Creation of a Superhero*, unpublished manuscript, 1976,12–13.

2 Arnold Goldsmith, *The Golem Remembered, 1909-1980: Variations of a Jewish Legend* (Wayne State University Press, 1981), 22.

3 This is a radical change in the legend and does not appear until the seventeenth century. Originally the legend concerned a warning against idolatry and man's attempt to make an artificial being, thus emulating God. See *The Golem Remembered*, 16–17.

4 Superman battled the golem in two comic book stories, "The Man who Murdered the Earth," *Superman* #248 (February, 1972) and a sequel that appeared in *Superman* # 258 (November, 1972).

5 Sharon Gillerman, "Samson in Vienna: The Theatrics of Jewish Masculinity," Jewish Social Studies 9:2 (Winter, 2003), 65.

6 Ibid.

7 Sharon Gillerman, "Strongman Siegmund Breitbart and Interpretations of the Jewish Body," in Michael Brenner and Gideon Reuveni, *Emancipation Through Muscles: Jews and Sports in Europe* (Lincoln: University of Nebraska Press, 2006), 63 .

Funnyman, Jewish Masculinity, and the Decline of the Superhero

By Thomas Andrae

Superman was the brainchild of two high school kids from Cleveland, Ohio, writer Jerry Siegel and artist Joe Shuster. They suffered five years of rejections from publishers until DC came out with a new magazine, *Action Comics* #1 (June, 1938), with Superman as the lead feature. Paid only $130 for the rights to the character, Siegel and Shuster lost millions when Superman became a marketing bonanza and an American icon. Most of us know about this fleecing. But we are unfamiliar with the story of a second fiasco: that of Funnyman, the superhero they hoped would become another Superman.

The seeds for Funnyman were sown when Siegel was drafted into the army in July 1943. Without Siegel aggressively protecting his and Shuster's rights, National Periodical Publications [later DC Comics] took over more and more control of production of Superman. Eventually Shuster lost his staff to National and became just another paid artist, whose poor eyesight made for a steadily diminishing workload. Siegel recalls this transformation in an interview with Phil Yeh in *Cobblestone* Magazine:

> I was under contract because I had signed a ten-year contract; this was one of the things that happened as time went by. While I was in the service they [National] started ghosting the Superman scripts, because obviously I couldn't write them while I was away in the service. At the same time, they took over Joe's end of it. Joe and I had a studio in Cleveland; Joe had artists working for him. When I went into the service, Joe and his staff went to New York, or at least some of them [the artists under Shuster's employ] did. I wasn't around and eventually most of Joe's workers worked directly for National instead of for Joe. When I came out of the service, I wanted to set up our studio again and operate the way we had before...and I encountered great resistance on that, and our troubles were on. [1]

Jerry Siegel and Joe Shuster, 1941.

In May 1947, Siegel and Shuster sued National for the rights to Superman, and for compensation for Superboy, which DC had published without Siegel's permission while he was away in the army. In May, 1948, the court awarded Siegel and Shuster $94,000 for the rights to Superboy, but gave National the rights to Superman.

While they were still working for National, Siegel and Shuster created another superhero, hoping they could strike gold a second time if things did not pan out with Superman. Funnyman was a radical departure from previous superheroes, a baggy-pants clown with a bulbous nose and oversized feet. He fought crime with gags, practical jokes, and a plethora of bizarre gadgets. One of the most outré superheroes ever created, the character never caught on and lasted only a scant six issues (January, 1948 to August, 1948), then faded into oblivion.

Fans and critics have dismissed Funnyman as a failed attempt to create another comics sensation, a Superman manqué. Thus, he has been written off as a kind of strange hybrid, an unfunny attempt to cross the superhero with humor comics. But Funnyman comic books and newspaper strips are so rare that most people have never read them and their significance has gone unaddressed. As we shall see, Funnyman was an emblem not only of a major shift in Siegel and Shuster's work, but also of important changes in the comic industry—and in the fate of the superhero. Funnyman, we shall argue, encoded a major departure from the macho masculinity that characterized Superman (and other superheroes) revealing the roots of the Man of Steel in ideas of Jewish masculinity that have been elided, and only recently acknowledged.[2]

Funnyman #1 laid out the character's origin. Larry Davis was a successful nightclub comedian who donned a clown costume and putty nose for a publicity stunt. But instead of capturing an actor, Davis subdued a real crook and liked the adventure so much that he assumed an alter ego as the clown-suited Funnyman. The character first appeared in a black-and-white ashcan edition in December 1947, apparently designed to secure Siegel and Shuster copyright of their character. Having signed away the rights to Superman they were determined not to lose another creation.

The Birth of Funnyman

Funnyman was the brainchild of Joe Shuster. "I remember when Joe got the idea," recalls Jean Shuster Peavy, Joe's sister. "Joe loved Danny Kaye and said, 'Boy, I'd love to do a comic strip with a Danny Kaye-type character.' The first time that we saw Danny was at the Paramount Theater in New York [in 1941]. Joe said that Danny was going to be a big star. That was before Danny was in films. He had been playing the Catskill Mountains and the summer resorts."[3]

Siegel took Shuster's idea and decided to turn the character into a superhero.

Funnyman #1: Origin Page.

According to a press release, "While Mr. Siegel was in the army, he thought of creating a new comic strip not solely on adventure lines, a vogue he considered waning." The new strip would be an innovation, "adventure combined with...comedy," recalling "the slapstick of the Keystone comedies, the thrills of Harold Lloyd films," and the "athletics of swashbuckling Douglas Fairbanks."

Siegel and Shuster discussed Funnyman with National Periodicals editor Whitney Ellsworth. Ellsworth was interested in the character but could not give Siegel and Shuster what they wanted: full ownership of *Funnyman* with the right to sell the feature to a newspaper syndicate and other licensors. National would agree to an income participation deal but had to retain control of editorial content and all subsidiary rights. The talks broke down in frustration. Behind the wheeling and dealing lay the fact that Siegel was nervous about signing a deal for Funnyman with a company he distrusted. In a letter to Siegel (February 3, 1947), DC publisher Jack Leibowitz wrote: "In your letter of January 27, you state that you are apprehensive about our being connected with your FUNNYMAN feature, and you quote our record of what you call 'flops.' The fact that Batman and Wonder Woman did not prosper as newspaper features does not detract from their value to us. So far as I am concerned, they are as valuable any day as Superman, and far less trouble to handle."

The tone was indicative of the growing acrimony between Siegel and DC management. "I never indicated that we would take your Funnyman feature," Leibowitz continued, "but as long as your ego tells you that anything you do must be a preordained success, I would be interested, just for the record, in having you name one feature—other than Superman—out of the numerous ones you've developed, which has enjoyed even a modicum of success." In a postscript to the letter to Leibowitz Siegel had written, "Why do you want to legally consider Funnyman? Why not brazenly take it, as you did Superboy?" Four months later Siegel and Shuster would file a lawsuit against DC.

Vin Sullivan was the first editor of *Action Comics* and was responsible for bringing the Man of Steel to National. He struck pay dirt again by suggesting to a young cartoonist named Bob Kane that he create another superhero for the company. The result was Batman. Sullivan had become disillusioned with National after seeing the way it treated Siegel and Shuster and decided to quit: "I didn't particularly like the way those people behaved," he recalled, "the way they did business."[4] In 1943 Sullivan founded Magazine Enterprise Comics (ME), a small offbeat company that produced Westerns, jungle comics, and crime comics, but few superheroes. Hearing of Siegel and Shuster's frustration with National he offered to work with them on any new project they wanted to bring him—including Funnyman. He even offered to give them the ownership deal they wanted, thinking that he might be able to publish the next Superman. Sullivan hoped to trade on their fame by emblazoning their names as the creators of Superman on the cover of *Funnyman* #1. However, with the lawsuit underway, National was not amused and demanded that Sullivan take the subtitle off the logo. Funnyman would have to make it on his own.

Funnyman has deep roots in Siegel and Shuster's lives. Some of their first collaborations had been humorous strips and it was the genre of comics they enjoyed most. "We both loved the comic strips," Siegel recalled, "it just so happened that the adventure stuff was what we managed to market, and that's what we did from there on."[5] Even before meeting Shuster,

Siegel and Shuster's first strongman hero, c. 1932.

Siegel had created a parody of Tarzan for Siegel's Cleveland high school newspaper, the *Glenville Torch*. It reveals Siegel's ambivalence about hyper-masculine heroes embodied later in the Superman-Clark Kent duality: "Just imagine the blonde young giant flying through the jungle. What a picture! What magnificence of form was his! Except for a dislocated hip, a broken arm, fallen arches, a twisted arm and a missing ear, he was the model of physical perfection." [6] In a sequel (Oct. 1, 1931), Siegel even lampooned muscleman ads that promised vigorous physical exercise could turn a weakling into a muscular Adonis. "If I take breathing exercises one hundred times a day for one hundred years," Goober tells himself, "I'll have the greatest chest in existence," pounding his pecs like Tarzan then falling into a coughing fit. Goober had troubles with an over-protective mother, Oolala, the Lion, just like Siegel whose mother worried about whether her impractical son would be able to make his way in the world. Lasting only two episodes, Goober became so popular that Siegel took to calling himself Jerry (Goober the Mighty) Siegel in the *Torch*.

Siegel had a suppressed desire to write comedy throughout his life. On September 9, 1938, close to the cover date of the first appearance of Superman (June 1938), he copyrighted a book with the Library of Congress. Written with Joe Shuster's brother Frank, it was a correspondence course titled *How to be Funny, a Practical Course of Serious Study in Creative Humor*. 134 pages long, it consisted of ten installments: Lesson One: Your Sense of Humor; Lesson Two: The Psychology of Humor; Lesson Three: Fundamentals of Wit and Humor; Lesson Four: The Types and Forms of Humor; Lesson Five: How to Originate Humor; Lesson Six: Examples of Humor Writing; Lesson Eight: The Art of Laughing; Lesson Nine: Material Advantages of Humor; Lesson Ten: The Professional Humorist. The entries indicate that Siegel had developed an analytical perspective not only on the mechanisms and types of humor but also on the job of being a humorist. Appropriately, he would make a professional comedian into a protagonist, Larry Davis, Funnyman's alter ego.

Siegel was an inveterate comedian who amused his classmates with his smart-alec humor and got in trouble with library personnel by making wisecracks while people tried to read. He was also a practical joker. "I remember Jerry would say, 'Hey how can we get people's attention,'" recalls Jean Shuster Peavy. Siegel would point to the sky and say, "'Look! What is it? What's up there?' He was a prankster, you know, there was nothing up there.... So he would make it seem like there was." [7] Siegel carried over this prankster humor into the first Superman stories. In *Action Comics* #1, for example, he recycled a gag that he had invented for a detective satire in the *Torch* that never appeared: Superman runs along a power line dragging a terrified villain and wisecracks: "Birds sit on the telephone wires and they don't get electrocuted—not unless they touch a telephone pole and are **grounded**! Oops! Almost touched that pole!"

Being small and timid, Siegel used aggressive and mocking humor in his writing to give him an authority he did not possess in real life. Frequently victimized by bigger classmates, he would conquer them in his daydreams and occasionally in schoolyard battles when he would playact the role of the media heroes he admired. Such confrontations gave Siegel a lifelong antipathy to bullies. Like his author, Funnyman fought physically imposing and more powerful foes with jokes and wisecracks, coupled with (often inept) derring-do.

The Body Politic

Siegel and Shuster have been described as classic nerds: bespectacled, unathletic, and shy around girls. [8] Clark Kent was their alter ego. Kent was timid, bespectacled, cowardly, and unattractive to women—and a writer, a quasi-intellectual. Superman was his antithesis—brave, strong, and handsome—a man of action, not words. While Superman was worshipped by Lois Lane, she ignored or reviled Kent, thinking him a "worm." The superhero body represents in graphic detail the muscularity, confidence, and power of the ideal of phallic masculinity. Superman can fly at supersonic speeds, see through walls, and even travel to other planets. Kent, his alter ego—which must be kept hidden—depicts the softness, powerlessness, and insecurity associated with the feminized male. However, Kent only pretends to be weak and cowardly; Superman is his real self—a symbol of the power that presumably lies within the weak and ineffectual ordinary man.

The Jewish male has traditionally epitomized the image of weak, timid manhood. As Paula Hyman notes, Jewish men have often been stereotyped as feminized: "...many Gentile observers of Jewish life in the late nineteenth and early twentieth centuries depicted male Jews in terms more often ascribed to women. Particularly in the industrialized West, Jewish men, even though assimilated to Western culture, were seen as unmanly." [9] While the Jewish brain was revered as the glory of Western civilization, the Jewish body was considered small, weak, and, in anti-Semitic stereotypes, degenerate and unhealthy. Writes Maurice Berger: "It was precisely this desexualized, ambivalent body that underlay the understanding of the Jew in the arts and science of the late ninetieth and early twentieth centuries. Indeed, in almost all 'legitimate' medical and biological discussions of pathology from 1880 to 1930, Jews represented the absolute negation of Aryan health and purity. Even Sigmund Freud's own understanding of the construction of gender to some extent appropriated these paradigms of the feminized Jewish body." [10]

However, to fully understand the duality between weakness and strength embodied

Earliest known drawing of Clark Kent, c. 1934–1935

by Kent and Superman, we must view it not just as an opposition between two character types but as a contrast between two ethics in Jewish culture that goes back centuries. As Paul Breines points out, between the destruction of the ancient Jewish state and the defeat of Jewish armed resistance to Roman power in the second century A.D. and the founding of Israel in 1948, Jews were not merely stateless, they were a people largely, often completely, excluded from landownership, farming, hunting, and war—from much of the world of effective bodily activity. He writes: "Europe's Jews had been bound to the sphere of circulation and commerce—the sphere of money, cunning, and abstraction. They were denied admission into the worlds of material production and violence, though as victims, they entered the latter world in droves." [11] As a consequence, claims Breines, Jews made a virtue of this historic necessity by constructing a remarkable culture of meekness, physical frailty, and gentleness, "a pale slouched identity nurtured in the stale air of their exclusion from the worlds of work and war."[12] One can hear echoes of this ethic in Clark Kent telling bullies that he "hates violence" and refusing to fight, only to redeem himself by ripping off his civilian clothes and, in Superman garb, to give the tough a thrashing. Behind the identity of gentleness and meekness Jewish males fantasized about expressing a tougher, stronger identity.

Because images of tough Jews had been marginalized, when Jews sought to counter the stereotype of Jewish weakness and gentleness they often turned to a non-Jewish model of manhood and the body.[13] The cult of the tough Jew as an alternative to Jewish frailty and gentleness rests on Aryan images of strength and masculinity which were also idealized by anti-Semites. Superman, and other superheroes, were modeled on the ancient Greek and Roman gods.[14] Siegel created the final version of Superman one night late in 1934 when, unable to sleep, he conjured up "a character like Samson, Hercules, and all the strong men I ever heard of rolled into one only more so."[15] Indeed, Superman wore sandals similar to those of classical strongmen, rather than boots, when he first appeared. His triangular-shaped body (broad shoulders and small waist), strong legs, and heavy musculature were inspired by images of bodybuilders emulating gods from classical antiquity that Joe Shuster absorbed from bodybuilding magazines when he practiced the sport as a youth.

These images of masculinity invoke a body politics, a grammar of body types in which idealized body images are conflated with the psychological and moral virtues that presumably inhere in them: courage, self-sacrifice, patriotism, and above all manliness. Physique presumably determines, or is evidence of, human nobility and virtue–although they have no intrinsic connection. At the same time, those bodies which do not fit the ideal are denigrated as not only physically lacking but morally and biologically inferior. This duality goes back to the ancient Greeks. Writes Kenneth Dutton: "In Greek society, physical imperfection was a subject of shame. Deformity, weakness or the degeneration of age tended to be looked upon with little sympathy or compassion."[16] Although few had the attributes of the classical physique, men would consider themselves deficient for not conforming to it, especially Jewish men.

Appearing in comic books, Charles Atlas promised the reader a transformation from a "98-lb weakling" to a "Greek God."

Ideals of the body are relative to different cultures. Dutton points out the contrast between Greek and Oriental ideals in this regard. Where athletes were worshipped as heroes in ancient Greece heroes became represented as athletes. With a bulging chest and muscular abdomen, Hercules is the archetype of the Greek god. Such images are those of warrior heroes engaged in conflicts with and conquest over others and over external nature. They are gods of great deeds and vigorous action. In contrast Oriental divinities like the Buddha are often depicted as sitting and inactive, engaged in contemplation and an interior journey into the self rather than external conquest, and have soft, round bellies, even potbellies, and no pronounced musculature, as in sculptures of the laughing, happy Buddhas which represent prosperity and good fortune. This plurality of body ideals reveals the body fascism that men have been subjected to in Western culture.

"We were aliens," comments Jewish cartoonist Jules Feiffer, "We didn't choose to be mild-mannered, bespectacled, and self-effacing. We chose to be bigger, stronger, blue-eyed and sought after by blond cheerleaders. Their cheerleaders. We chose to be *them*."[17] Superman, and the superhero, thus represented "the ultimate at assimilationist fantasy," according to Feiffer. "The mild manners and glasses that signified a class of nerdy Clark Kents was in no way, our real truth. Underneath that smucky face there lived Men of Steel."[18] Comic book creators anglicized their names so that they sounded more "American."

WHEN THE DICTATOR'S GUARDS OFFER OPPOSITION, THEY FIND THE LONE INTRUDER TOO MUCH FOR THEM!
KILL THE SWINE! DON'T LET HIM TOUCH ME!
I'LL GET AROUND TO YOU IN A FEW SECONDS!

I'D LIKE TO LAND A STRICTLY NON-ARYAN SOCK ON YOUR JAW, BUT THERE'S NO TIME FOR THAT! YOU'RE COMING WITH ME WHILE I VISIT A CERTAIN PAL OF YOURS.
PUT ME DOWN! YOU'RE HURTING ME!

EASTWARD RACES SUPERMAN WITH HIS UNWILLING BURDEN, AT A CLIP THAT WOULD OUTDISTANCE THE FASTEST PLANE ....!
DON'T FIRE! HE'S HOLDING THE FUEHRER HOSTAGE!

MOSCOW, RUSSIA— AS STALIN REVIEWS HIS TROOPS FROM ATOP A BALCONY, THE MAN OF STEEL'S FIGURE PLUMMETS FROM THE SKY PLUCKING HIM FROM HIS PERCH...

JOE, MEET ADOLF!
WHAT-??

AS SUPERMAN RACES INTO THE MASSED MARCHERS, THE TROOPS SCATTER IN CONFUSION!
THAT'S RIGHT! CLEAR THE WAY!

WHERE ARE YOU TAKING US?
NEXT STOP— GENEVA, SWITZERLAND!

LATER— SUPERMAN DROPS IN ON A MEETING OF THE LEAGUE OF NATIONS...
GENTLEMEN, I'VE BROUGHT BEFORE YOU THE TWO POWER-MAD SCOUNDRELS RESPONSIBLE FOR EUROPE'S PRESENT ILLS. WHAT IS YOUR JUDGEMENT?

ADOLF HITLER AND JOSEF STALIN— WE PRONOUNCE YOU GUILTY OF MODERN HISTORY'S GREATEST CRIME — UNPROVOKED AGGRESSION AGAINST DEFENSELESS COUNTRIES.

Bob Kahn, creator of Batman, changed his name to Bob Kane, Captain America artist Jack Kurtzberg adopted the Irish-sounding nom de plume Jack Kirby, and Timely/Marvel scripter Stan Leibowitz became Stan Lee.

Attempting to cope with the demands of depression and war, Jews sought to change their image from nebbishy weaklings to tough street fighters. The transition from schlemiel to tough Jew is apparent in Siegel's explanation of why he created Superman:

> What led me into conceiving SUPERMAN in the early Thirties? Listening to President Roosevelt's 'fireside chats'...being unemployed and worried during the Depression and knowing hopelessness and fear. Hearing and reading of the oppression and slaughter of helpless, oppressed Jews in Nazi Germany...seeing movies depicting the horrors of privation suffered by the downtrodden...reading of gallant, avenging heroes in the pulps, and seeing equally crusading heroes on the screen in feature films and movie serials (often pitted against malevolent, grasping, ruthless madmen) I had the great urge to help...help the despairing masses, somehow." [ellipses in original]— And Superman, aiding the downtrodden and oppressed, has caught the imagination of a world. [19]

In a two-page story, "How Superman Would End the War" (*Look* magazine, February 27, 1940), Superman races to the Siegfried Line. "The Nazis claim that the West Wall is invulnerable—well here's where I find out!" he declares. Unable to stop him, the Germans panic as the Man of Steel destroys the artillery emplacement, yelling to French troops to "come and get 'em!" Going to Germany he rips off the top of Hitler's retreat and abducts the cowering dictator. Then Superman flies to Russia and grabs Stalin, taking both dictators to the League of Nations to be tried for war crimes. The judge finds the two scoundrels guilty of "unprovoked aggression against defenseless countries." The story also reveals a pacifist ethos: Hitler and Stalin had started World War II by invading other nations. Superman brings the tyrants responsible for this aggression to the world court, using the rule of law to resolve international conflicts rather than violence. Siegel's pacifist ethos first surfaced in *Action Comics* #2 where he showed that foreign wars are perpetrated only to bring profits to munitions manufacturers.

The *Look* tale was one of Siegel's favorites and expressed a fantasy greatly desired by an America not yet at war—to halt the Nazi blitzkrieg. But it is something of an anomaly: Superman can easily end the war without readers questioning it because the conflict was safely distant. But this would have seemed ridiculous once American fighting forces were suffering and dying. Because Superman's power is so great, an unstated question in wartime stories was why he didn't just end the war, and this threatened to undermine the whole fantasy of omnipotence and invulnerability that the character was premised upon. Thus, to maintain a semblance of realism, it was rare to see Superman take on the Nazis in any Superman stories, although Superman's editors would splash scenes of Superman battling the Axis on many comic book covers. Most stories with Nazi villains dealt with the German American Bund and the threat of espionage in the U.S., or allegorical stories in which Superman takes on Hitler-like tyrants in fictional European countries.[20]

The *Look* story was one of Siegel's recurrent diatribes against bullies in which he portrayed the bellicose Hitler as a cowardly crybaby. It brought a sharp rebuke from Nazi

Minister of Propaganda Josef Goebbels who attacked both Superman and his Jewish writer, whom Goebbels denounced in the April 25, 1940 issue of *Das Schwartze Korps*, weekly paper of the S.S.:

> Jerry Siegel, an intellectually and physically circumcised chap who has his headquarters in New York, is the inventor of a colorful figure with...an overdeveloped body and an underdeveloped mind, 'Superman'.... As you can see, there is nothing the Sadducees won't do for money! Jerry Siegellack stinks. Woe to the American youth, who must live in such a poisoned atmosphere and don't even notice the poison they swallow daily.

Although Siegel's identity as a Jew was fairly well known, Superman's role as a Jewish hero was always masked, and in appearance he was a Gentile hero modeled after Hollywood action heroes and comic-strip tough guys. But, there were Jewish accents to the Man of Steel that scholars have recently begun to address: his role as a messiah aiding the oppressed, his immigrant status and exile from his a homeland where his race was destroyed, his Moses-like origin as an abandoned babe, even his black hair have been interpreted as signifiers of his hidden ethnicity.[21] Kryptonite (the metal from Superman's home planet which robbed him of his strength) too can be viewed through a Jewish prism: to assimilating Jews, the hold of the old country was perceived as something to avoid, a weakness that disempowered them in America and could provoke anti-Semitism. The goal was to make one's ethnicity invisible, not to reveal it to the world. There were also the seeming Jewish allusions in Superman's father's name, Jor-El, "El" being the Hebrew word for God. However, as Siegel himself explained: "the name 'Jor-l' is an anagram of my name, Jerome Siegel."[22] Yet, he admitted that he might have been unconsciously aware of the Jewish associations when he created the Kryptonian name.

In the late nineteenth and early twentieth centuries, only genetically pure heroes like Tarzan could represent the highest form of human evolution. At this time Anglo-American culture was in the grip of Social Darwinism, which proclaimed the existence of superior and inferior races and glorified the WASP lineage. Created at a time when Jews were able to more freely assimilate into American culture, Superman is an immigrant and this represents an important change in the notion that only Anglo-Saxons could be powerful symbols of masculine prowess and human perfection. This change was made possible by broadening the definition of what constituted whiteness to include Jewish immigrants.[23]

World War II marked the zenith of the melting pot ideal for Americans of European origin. By the 1940s, the flood tide of immigration from Europe had diminished and groups once perceived as having the potential for having their loyalty to foreign nations questioned were increasingly composed of second- and third-generation immigrants. Instead of mass xenophobia and cultural repression, white ethnic groups were welcomed with open arms in wartime campaigns for national unity, which promoted the unification of Americans of different national backgrounds and celebrated the contributions of immigrant groups to America. This attempt to build wartime unity was the precursor of a different vision of America which "for the first time included white ethnic Americans in the charmed circle of full-fledged Americans."[24]

Ironically, both Jews and anti-Semites aspired to the same ideal of hyper-masculinity. In patriarchal society, male identity has traditionally been defined in terms of self-sufficiency, toughness, competitiveness, and power. This form of masculinity requires the subordination of women and posits as deviant and unnatural women who are overly masculine, gay men, and feminized males. Both superheroes and bodybuilders represent ideals that assume this type of heterosexism. According to Susan Bordo: "Muscles have chiefly symbolized and continue to symbolize masculine power as physical strength frequently operating as a means of coding the 'naturalness' of sexual difference." The hyper-masculine male epitomizes what Klaus Theweleit calls the armored body, prepresented in the fantasies of the proto-Nazi Freikorps.[25] In masculinist psychology, body and psyche are united in erecting a psychic armor that defends against "feminine" weakness, emotional vulnerability, and softness, modes of expression that must be controlled by the rational, dominant male.

Superman's physical invulnerability is mirrored by an emotional rigidity, his muscular armoring masking an emotional armor. As Siegel put it: "I figured that the character would be so advanced that he would be invulnerable in other ways than physically."[26] In a revenge of the nerds, Siegel secretly enjoyed the fact "that women, who just didn't care about somebody like Clark Kent, would go ape over somebody like Superman," but he would be unaffected by all their admiration.[27] "A big inside joke [on Lois] was that the fellow she cared about was the fellow whom she loathed," Siegel explained, making her look ridiculous because she was unable to see the real man within.[28] Superman kept totally removed from emotional involvement with Lois or any other women during the Thirties and Forties, distancing himself from the anxieties surrounding intimacy and vulnerability. Thus, he would never give in to the temptations of his love for Lois for, in patriarchal ideology, this would be a threat to his autonomy and power and would domesticate him.

The ideal of hyper-masculinity in Superman dichotomizes males, polarizing them into exaggerated extremes: either you are muscled, brave, and handsome or you are weak, cowardly, and plain with nothing in between. However, it is important to see that the strength/weakness binary does not really imply opposites but inversions that depend on each other. As Feiffer puts it, Clark Kent was Superman's idea of what ordinary men are really like: they are scared, incompetent, and powerless—and klutzes with women. However, ordinary males only look weak, unattractive, and cowardly if one accepts the super-powerful alpha male as the ideal of masculinity.

The Schlemiel and the Tough Jew

Male psychology is more complex than this dichotomizing vision allows: men actually experience both a fear of and desire for feminization and vulnerability, a longing for love and attachment as well as traditional male desires for autonomy, dominance, and self-sufficiency. This ambivalence was encoded into the strange ménage à trois between Superman, Clark Kent, and Lois Lane. As Feiffer observes, there is a puzzle at the heart of the Superman-Clark Kent duality. Kent loves and pursues Lois but is bullied and rejected by her. As Superman he rebuffs her advances yet shows an inordinate concern for rescuing and protecting her. Since Superman and Kent are supposedly the same person this behavior demands an explanation. In numerous stories Kent expresses the desire that Lois love him for himself, i.e. as Kent. Since this would mean loving a fake, fabricated personality it makes no sense. The only logical conclusion is that Kent is not merely a put-on and Superman the true identity but that both identities are aspects of a single personality each autonomous in their own realms. There is thus a schizoid relationship between Kent and Superman. Siegel's genius was to make Kent an intrinsic part of Superman's identity which could not be shorn as the "feminine" parts of the self are exhorted to be in Theweleit's notion of the fascist armored body.

Kent's desire that Lois love him in his Kent role can be seen as a submerged desire, marginalized in the stories, that Lois love him for his vulnerable self and not always for his strong, heroic identity. This impulse comes out in postwar stories (often written by Siegel) in which Superman becomes involved in intense romances with women (in imaginary and time-travel tales which do not undermine the usual formula), and finally marries Lois in the 1980s.[29] He even ages and dies in one imaginary tale.[30] Siegel had always wanted Superman to be a more vulnerable character and wrote the first story in which the Man of Steel loses his powers due to exposure to Kryptonite, but his editors rejected it.[31] Significantly, in this story Superman reveals his identity to Lois for the first time and agrees to become partners with her in fighting crime. This would have made for more sexual equality in the series and made Lois a more developed character.

Funnyman can be interpreted as an expression of Siegel's desire to create a more human, more vulnerable character. This allowed Siegel to affirm the disavowed, "Jewish" side of the Kent identity, but without the dyslogistic connotations of weakness and ineffectuality associated with it. Funnyman represents an inversion of Superman's hyper-masculinity. Larry Davis, Funnyman's "true" identity, is a rich and highly successful nightclub comedian who is worshipped by the public and loved by his beautiful manager, June Farrell, a Lois Lane look-alike. Indeed, June's last name was inspired by actress Glenda Farrell, whose tough-talking reporter role, Torchy Blaine, was one of the inspirations for Lois.[32] However, Funnyman radically departed from the Superman strip. Unlike Superman's alter ego Clark Kent, Davis is not defined as a weakling and "worm" by the woman he loves. The Superman-Kent-Lois Lane triangle does not exist in the Funnyman universe. Rather, Davis is a relatively handsome, WASP male while Funnyman is a feminized, deviant male who wears a clown suit, has a spindly body, and sports a prominent putty nose rather than being a handsome Adonis like the conventional superhero. Funnyman is thus placed in the position of Kent as the anti-heroic male figure.

Unlike Superman, Funnyman is always weaker than his opponents who take the form of burly, muscular bullies like those that terrorize Clark Kent in early Superman stories. In *Funnyman #4*, for example, Funnyman is transported back to the Middle Ages and must fight a giant knight who threatens to kill him. Unlike Superman who relies on brawn to quell his opponents, Funnyman defeats villains through the use of his wits (and an assorted number of eccentric technological gadgets à la Batman). His powers are those of the weak, again putting him into the position of the feminized male.

In a further inversion of the superhero myth, Funnyman is often portrayed as none too bright and ends up making foolish mistakes. In *Funnyman* # 1, for example, he chases the teen terrors who have stolen his valuable antique watch. But he discovers that he has risked his life for nothing since June has replaced the watch with a cheap imitation and tried to inform him of the switch but the hero would not take the time to listen to her. Funnyman's triumph goes hand in hand with his ineptitude, as appropriate for his clown persona, and Larry Davis laughs hysterically at his inanity. This is totally contrary to the image of the seemingly omnipotent Superman of the Golden Age comics.

Popular culture often functions to hide the contents of repressed elements that form the absent center around which they revolve. As Gary Engle observes, Superman is an archetypal figure of the immigrant and was an alien from another planet who must assimilate himself into American culture.[33] Funnyman is an emblem of the Jewish immigrant that was at the center of the Superman mythos that was never overtly visible. The prominent nose, baggy pants, and outré look and manners of the character are an analogue of the immigrant and more particularly an allusion to the stereotype of the Jewish immigrant of the period.

The clown hero can also be seen as a transformed version of the Jewish schlemiel—the timid, emasculated, ineffectual character embodied by Clark Kent. Gender is not merely a description of sexuality and sexual difference but also a way of constructing relationships of power. By caricaturing Jewish men as feminized, anti-Semites deprived them of the power and honor assumed to be theirs as men, leading Jews to hide their ethnicity. In a volte-face, Funnyman exposed more of Siegel's Jewish identity. First of all, the character's identification as a comedian who fought more powerful villains with jokes and puns rather than brawn suggested his Jewishness and the long association of Jews with comedy. Siegel also used humorous Yiddishisms in his stories: one Funnyman story features a character named Noodnik Nogoodnik, the latter word being Yiddish slang for a worthless, disreputable, or malicious person.[34] Most importantly, the character was based on Jewish comedian Danny Kaye. The superhero has his red hair, large nose, and skinny body. He also has his manic sensibility. Kaye's humor was grounded in hysterical activity, making him an apt inspiration for a humorous action hero. However, this character psychology also reveals his hidden Jewishness: along with their feminization Jews have often been stereotyped as neurotic hysterics, as the Woody Allen film persona attests.

Kaye was one of the most popular comedians of the 1940s and became a major star in a series of feature films. He was the son of immigrants and developed a comedy routine out of mugging, scat singing, and mangled speech, a disguised allusion to the stereotype of Jewish immigrants' Yiddish inflections of English words and incapacity to speak the language fluidly. Assimilation was the key cultural agenda of Jews of the period and media producers were keen on disguising hints of ethnic particularity believing that it could harm their popularity if actors were not seen as WASPs. Thus Samuel Goldwyn, himself a Jew, ordered Kaye to dye his hair blond and get a nose job because Kaye "looked too Jewish."[35] Although Kaye had his hair dyed for his first major film, *Up in Arms* (1944), he reverted to

In contrast to Superman, Funnyman faced overwhelming odds, both physical and sexual. (*Funnyman #5*, 1948).

red locks in later features. More importantly, he refused to have a nose job.

Ironically, Larry Davis, Funnyman's "real" self, has the nose job that Kaye refused, while Funnyman sports the Jewish comedian's large shnoz. Funnyman thus can be interpreted as a visual symbol of the repressed Jewish male identity of the superhero made visually manifest. However, unlike the appendage of the stereotypical image of the Jewish male, Funnyman's nose is only a putty attachment and can be discarded at will, allowing the superhero to become the WASPish-looking Larry Davis. The comedian's real self is thus the conventionally handsome Davis rather than the ethnic Other. Although this normalizes Davis' appearance allowing him to fit in with conventional comic book heroes, Funnyman remains a grotesque and outré figure for a superhero, a major reason for the public's immediate and continuing dislike of the character.

There were other carryovers from Danny Kaye's filmic persona into the Funnyman strip. Kaye was noted for having both a sexually ambiguous on-screen and off-screen image. He was rumored to have had a ten-year affair with legendary actor Laurence Olivier.[36] Kaye's sexual ambiguity is evident in the film *Up in Arms* where he does part of a musical sequence in drag. But Kaye's screen persona exemplified more endemic gender-bending. In *The Secret Life of Walter Mitty* (1947) and other films, he played characters that had dual identities. Mitty was a meek, henpecked bookworm who fantasized he was a bold, heroic adventurer. The dual identity must have had a strong attraction for Siegel since it replicated the Superman-Kent formula. Mitty even worked as a writer for a publisher of sensationalistic pulp magazines filled with sex and gore who abused and exploited him, much like DC publishers Jack Leibowitz and Harry Donenfeld whom Siegel worked for.

The Decline of the Superhero

The creation of an anti-hero like Funnyman was made possible by the decline of the traditional superhero and the hyper-masculinity he embodied. Indeed, Siegel's press release for Funnyman reveals that he was well aware of the "waning" of the traditional superhero and positioned Funnyman as an alternative. Superman was created during the Depression as a superbly indomitable force who represented popular desires for social change. He could prevent mine owners from exploiting workers, unscrupulous munitions manufacturers from fomenting a phony war, and extinguish juvenile delinquency. His Jewish creators had invented a eugenically perfect being as a counter-symbol to the Nazi's ideology of the master race and the perpetuation of anti-Semitic oppression. Superman, and the superhero generally, thus could readily be recast as an indomitable patriotic hero. A legion of superhero imitators conducted a bloody war against the Axis powers in order to protect freedom and democracy. Comics' sales boomed during wartime with Superman leading the pack, selling more than a million comic books per month.

Although Superman could end a war single-handedly, in 1940 the actual experiences of war made the notion of an invulnerable, omnipotent hero increasingly questionable. Indeed, during the early years of the conflagration it was not clear that America was going to win and possible that fascism, not democracy, would triumph. As the cost of winning the war—in millions of lives, mangled bodies, wartime atrocities, and psychological trauma-became apparent the triumphalist vision of the superhero became less palatable. Patriotism had been the driving force behind the boom in superheroes during the war. With the Allied victory in 1945 and the conclusion of hostilities superheroes had been robbed of much of their raison d'être. Over seven hundred superheroes had been created during the war and the genre's success peaked with 40 titles in 1944. Each succeeding year saw a progressive drop in sales: 33 titles in 1945, 28 in 1946, 19 in 1947, 14 in 1948, eight in 1949, and only four in 1950–1951.[37] Poor sales compelled publishers to either cancel superhero titles or transform them into comic books in other genres. Thus, *All-American Comics,* the home of Green Lantern, became *All-American Men of War,* and *All Star Comics,* featuring a superhero group, became *All Star Western.*

The decline of the superhero had already been prefigured by developments during the war years. By 1943, for example, sales of *Superman* comics had been eclipsed by *Captain Marvel Adventures* as the bestselling comic book in America. Captain Marvel was a parody of the superhero whose most famous villain was Mr. Mind, a worm, bent on world domination like Hitler. Trying to emulate the success of its rival, Superman comics began to take a more humorous view of macho masculinity in the late-war and postwar years, evident in a distinctive transformation of the title's covers. Issues of Superman comics during the early Forties showed an omnipotent god demolishing the pillars of a building

SUPERMAN
No.30
SEPT.-OCT...TEN CENTS
A SUPERMAN PUBLICATION
DC
IND
SUPERMAN
REG U S PAT OFF
What's This ?!?
LOIS LANE GIVES SUPERMAN
THE GO-BY FOR CLARK KENT?!?
READ
"SUPERMAN ALIAS SUPERMAN"
SNAP!

Mr. Mxyztpik taunts Superman in this splash page from the imp's first appearance in comic books (*Superman* #30, 1944).

as his archrival Luthor fled in terror (#4), ripping the steel bars from a bank to rescue the people imprisoned within (#5), attacking a Nazi ship as it is about to attack a boatload of innocent civilians (#13), and holding Hitler and Tojo by the scruffs of their necks while he stands astride the world (#17). By the mid-Forties these images of spectacular power were supplanted by a series of humorous covers such as Lois Lane rejecting a quizzical Superman for a date with a bemused Clark Kent (#30), a henpecked Superman being chastised by Lois Lane for stealing food from the refrigerator and leaving a mess on the floor (#36), and Superman nervously cranking up an antique car driven by an old harridan stopped at a stop sign while a cop looks on angrily (#46)—suggesting Superman was as domesticated and emasculated as the ordinary male.

The change in Superman's masculine status mirrored that of his creators. Although Siegel and Shuster had created Superman as a symbol of masculine autonomy, dominance, and strength, the two creators were increasingly mistreated by their editors and publisher, and shared little of Superman's vaunted power. Ellsworth attacked Siegel's stories and Shuster's art and even threatened to replace them if the feature did not improve. And the publisher's promises of increased revue from sharing in merchandizing profits either went unfulfilled or met with token payments. Although they had created one of the most popular fictional characters of all time, Siegel and Shuster had become victims of their own creation's success.

Siegel left hints of his dissatisfaction in his stories. In "King of the Comic Books" (*Superman* #25, 1943), one of the last stories he wrote before being drafted, Siegel parodied Superman as a buck-toothed oaf named Geezer who has "taken the public by storm." Henry Jones, his author, is a small, timid artist who looks remarkably like Joe Shuster. When Kent asks him how he produces so many Geezer comics Jones shows him a room full of writers and another room filled with artists. Jones himself is reduced to the ignominy of answering stacks of fan mail, reflecting Siegel's angst at his editor's increasing control of Superman and fear that, while he was in the army, the company would take over complete production of the Superman line. The Man of Steel tells Jones: "a comic character's continued popularity is governed by the amount of care a creator puts into his conception." Disguised as Geezer, Superman chides Jones for not giving the superhero his best and letting others do his work for him, an implicit swipe at DC editors for taking control of Superman away from his creators, and forces Jones to take charge of the strip. "Geezer is better than ever," Lois exudes to Clark, "Henry Jones seems a man inspired!" alluding to the increased quality that would accrue to Superman if his creators had control over the strip.

By the mid-Forties, Siegel was populating his stories with three humorous supervillains who taunted Superman: The Toyman, The Prankster, and Mr. Mxyztplk. These new characters prefigured Siegel's creation of Funnyman and recapitulated the way Siegel had previously changed Superman from being a villain into a hero. Mxyztplk was the most important of the new villains. Inspired by Bugs Bunny, and Al Capp's Joe Blyfstyk (a little man with a black cloud perpetually over his head who brought misfortune to all those around him), Mxyztplk was a trickster figure who was an imp from the fifth dimension and initially not a criminal per se. His raison d'être was to create havoc and to humiliate Superman. Siegel was getting tired of Superman's infallibility and introduced the scamp as "a welcome change of pace" who would make "the noble idol of millions uncomfortable on his super-pedestal."[38]

Superman had originally been an outlaw who fought social injustice and aided the oppressed. But Siegel's publishers demanded that the Man of Steel operate inside the law and fight criminals rather than social evils.[39] Feeling "regimented" by his editors, Siegel was able to indulge in the anarchistic behavior he enjoyed by having the imp make a fool of Superman—and other authority figures. Inverting the message of bodybuilding ads, Mxyztplk is short, bald, and puny (an image of both the stereotypical weak Jew and of Siegel himself) and in his comic book debut mocks the attempts of muscle-bound lifeguards to rescue him (*Superman* #30, 1944). Clearly the ideal of hyper-masculinity and patriotism represented by the superhero was in disrepair.

Funnyman continued some of Mxyztplk's animus to authority and recaptured intimations of the early Superman's lawlessness and outlaw status. A recurring character is a dim-witted Irish cop named Sgt. Harrigan. The clown repeatedly ridicules the policeman and makes him look foolish, and he functions much like the Keystone Kops on which Funnyman was partially based. In "The Super Snooper" (*Funnyman #6*), for example, Harrigan tries to handcuff Funnyman to prevent him from interfering in police business. But Funnyman twists his wrists around so that the cop ends up handcuffing himself instead, and the "super snooper" blithely goes about solving the crime. As revenge, Harrigan threatens to arrest him for being a public nuisance. However, like Mxyztplk, Funnyman functions as a trickster figure who can always outsmart a more powerful foe: he reminds Harrigan that if he does arrest him the public will learn of the embarrassing episode of the handcuffs and his superiors will discover that someone else solved the case. Thus, Harrigan must let him go. Nevertheless, Funnyman's battles against law and order remain limited to scuffles with a lone cop, and he never evolves into an anti-establishment hero who fights the rich and powerful like the early Superman.

Comic Book Noir

In the postwar era superheroes were supplanted by a number of genres including crime, romance, horror, Westerns, and funny animals. These changes heralded the biggest sales boom in comic book history fueled by the Baby Boom, which had begun in 1946. Comics were able to sustain an uninterrupted growth in sales peaking in 1952 when approximately one billion magazines representing more than thirty-one hundred titles were published. [40] After that year comics increasingly declined in popularity as the new medium of television began to displace them as forms of domestic entertainment. Fueling the decline, the institution of the Comics Code in 1954, one of the most restrictive censorship codes of any mass medium, decimated the industry, and it never could recover its previous level of popularity.

During the postwar years American popular culture evidenced two competing trends. On the surface was a glow of optimism and triumphalism. America had not only won the war but also achieved economic world dominance, as much of Europe and Asia lay in rubble while our nation was left unscathed. The period also saw the beginnings of a mass migration to suburbia and the rebirth of a consumer–driven society. Beneath the surface, however, American culture exhibited an anxious, pessimistic, and paranoid mood exemplified in the popularity of film noir, which played to the period's darker concerns. Film noir showcased postwar disillusionment focusing on doomed anti-heroes and seductive and treacherous femmes fatales. Comic books followed suit. In the years that *Funnyman* appeared crime was one of the most popular genres of comic books. From 1948 to 1949 nearly one in every seven comic books sold in America was a crime comic book. Crime comics embodied a postwar appetite for hard-edged, "realistic" entertainment. Crime and gangster pictures like *The Killers* (1946) and *Dillinger* (1945) were shot in a quasi-documentary style and crime comics followed suit, claiming to be documentary accounts of real-life crimes and the exploits of infamous criminals. Crime comic books came to prominence after American servicemen (a quarter of whom had been regular comic book readers) returned to civilian life. Older and more mature, such readers were no longer fascinated by adolescent fantasies of omnipotent superheroes fighting the Axis powers. Crime comics displayed a not-too-subtle critique of the American Dream and romantic bliss promised by popular Forties songs and films, evident in the sexism, fatalism, and pessimism of film noir. Instead of hard work and connubial bliss, crime comics glorified quick riches, brutality, and misogyny.

The crime comics craze was reflected in several issues of *Funnyman*. During the war and postwar years, experts and the general public came to believe that America was undergoing a wave of juvenile delinquency. Siegel and Shuster's "The Teen-Age Terror!" (*Funnyman* #1) features a spree of celebrity robberies. A Hollywood star's $10,000 mink scarf is taken; Honkie Sonota, a Frank Sinatra take-off, has his diamond ring stolen; and Larry Davis' heirloom watch is pilfered—all by teenage fans. Funnyman tracks down the gang and its adult crime lord and brings them to justice.

Siegel and Shuster also indirectly addressed crime comics in "The Peculiar Pacifier" (*Funnyman #5*). The story revolves around a hackneyed plot involving a mad scientist's invention of a pacifying gas that makes people "conciliatory." However, Siegel's real aim is to satirize crime comics. "For sheer gruesomeness and brutality," Larry tells June, "'Louie the Lout' is unsurpassed!" "It's amazing what the great American public will stand for in the name of 'humor,'" June replies. This is an implicit indictment of crime comics as passing for innocent kiddie fare. At the newspaper syndicate, we see that the artist is Karl Borisloff, a reference to horror film star Boris Karloff. The editor tells Karl: "You...have capitalized in your comic strip upon the mean and seamy aspects of life—murders, tortures, knifings, double-crosses...and you've always pictured them in almost clinical detail." But, he cautions, the public's taste has swung back to "clean, wholesome comic-strip heroes like 'Bringing up Brother' and 'Brunettie'," references to the family-oriented comic strips "Bringing up Father" and "Blondie." Siegel's mention of "comic-strip heroes" suggests that he believed that crime comics were crowding out the genre of superhero comics that he had invented.

The editor warns that the "Louie the Lout" strip is headed for "oblivion" unless Borisloff can come up with something more gruesome than ever before. Here Siegel satirizes the rush to the bottom of crime comics: their need to create increasingly more sensationalistic images of bloodshed to sell comics. Borisloff creates a story so awful that it only sells to a Boston daily (thanks to the aid of an accidental dose of the pacifier gas). The ending is ironic: The strip is cancelled in every one of the syndicates but the city noted for its puritanical restrictiveness, and Borisloff will never be able to live down his shame. But, the real shame, Siegel implies, is a comic industry that is catering to what he perceived as a sadistic and dangerous genre. Siegel was not alone in this feeling. 1947–1948 saw the rise of a vigorous anti-comics crusade. It was led by psychiatrist Fredric Wertham who accused comic books, and crime comics in particular, of fostering juvenile delinquency and other social pathologies. Wertham would become the leading voice in the anti-comic-book crusade of the 1950s which culminated in the comic book industry's adoption of the Comics Code.

Siegel always felt that other superheroes were pale copies of Superman and, in effect, had plagiarized the character. He testified to this in the 1939 trial in which DC Comics sued Fox Feature Syndicate, the company that produced the first Superman clone, Wonder Man. It was written and drawn by comics legend Will Eisner on the orders of his publisher to produce another Superman. In "Funman, Comicman, and Laffman" (*Funnyman #1*) Siegel lampooned copies of Funnyman as pale imitations. The clown kicks them in the behind and sends them to jail, scoffing, "Cheap imitations! Scram you bums!" Yet, beneath the bravado, Siegel was worried about what would happen to him and Shuster after losing Superman in their lawsuit with National and that they might end up has-beens. In "Super Schemer" (*Funnyman #6*) a crook named Schemer Beamer goes to prison in 1938, the year that Siegel and Shuster's Superman first appeared, and gets out of prison later only to find that his gang has become a bunch of losers and that he has lost his cache. His chief enforcer, Rockjaw, has developed a glass jaw, Cruncher has lost his death-grip, and Beamer's moll, "The Curve," has become plump and lost her power as a femme fatale. There have been a "lot of changes in the ten years since he has been away," she tells him. The ten-year reference had a portentous meaning for Superman's creators: Siegel and Shuster's contract ended ten years after The Man of Steel debuted, and they had lost Superman in a May 19, 1948 court decision. Siegel's intimation of impending doom would prove to be disquietingly prescient.

Funnyman also registered other important changes in postwar popular culture. A seismic shift in gender roles during the war years added to a sense of male malaise and made postwar readjustment especially difficult. During the war, women assumed jobs formerly occupied by men that were gender-coded as "masculine," becoming truck drivers, stevedores, and welders. After the war, women were supposed to relinquish their jobs to male veterans and return to the home. However, many women refused to give up their newfound freedom and independence, creating a destabilizing crisis in formerly naturalized definitions of masculinity and femininity. The femme fatale in film noir exemplified this crisis—a strong, sexually aggressive woman who refused to stay in her "proper," dependent place. The power of the femme fatale was attractive to women because she was able to display an assertiveness and agency that had been prohibited, but this also threatened traditional codes of masculinity. This threat was augmented by the increase in corporate power during the war, which critics feared was sapping male individualism and autonomy and making male employees into conformist organization men. Feelings of male lack and powerlessness were often projected onto scapegoats, especially women, and conflated with a fear of women's increasing power in the public sphere.

Superman editors thought this drawing of Lois Lane was too sexy for Superman readers (*Superman* #7, 1940)...

In the Thirties and Forties, Lois Lane had pursued Superman but never exerted a sexual hold on him, and he remained puritanical and asexual. This was no accident for DC editors followed a conscious policy of "de-sexing" Superman. DC publishers Jack Leibowitz and Harry Donenfeld had published porno magazines in the 1930s and Donenfeld had been indicted on obscenity charges. Thus, they were very skittish about complaints from public watchdogs about the sexual or violent content of their comic books and feared federal regulation. Although we associate the comics censorship crusade with the 1950s it really emerged at the same time as the superhero. Superman and Batman, for example, were viewed by various critics as violent vigilantes uncomfortably similar in their lawlessness to the fascist supermen of Germany. After Batman carried a gun in the late Thirties and used a machine gun to mow down monsters in *Batman #1* (Spring, 1940) DC Editor Whitney Ellsworth prohibited the Dark Knight from carrying a gun again or killing a criminal, and DC adopted a strict censorship code. Batman became an honorary policeman, and Superman could no longer operate outside the law and became a pro-social, establishment figure.

In a letter to Siegel from Whitney Ellsworth dated February 19, 1941, Ellsworth warns him "you know as well as I do what sort of censure we are up against." This time the problem was not violence but sex. Shuster had a penchant for drawing sexy women and a curvaceous Lois made Ellsworth anxious that moral watchdogs might complain. "[W]hy is it necessary to shade Lois' breasts and the underside of her tummy and the vertical pen-lines we can't understand. She looks pregnant. Murray suggests that you arrange for her to have an abortion or the baby and get it over with so that her figure can return to something a little more like the tasty dish she is supposed to be. She is much too stocky and much too unpleasantly sexy." The criticism did not stop with Lois. Ellsworth castigated Shuster for making Superman look gay or in the Forties slang of Ellsworth's letter, "lah-de-dah" with "a nice fat bottom."

In *Funnyman* Shuster finally got his chance to portray sexy women, indulging in the

...and objected to Shuster's rendition of a "gay" Superman (*Superman* comic strip, 1941).

postwar fascination with femmes fatales and the fatal male that was her victim. In "The Kute Knockout!" (*Funnyman #2*), for example, Doc Gimmick, a recurring villain in the series, invents a robot femme fatale who waits for male victims by striking a sexy pose under a streetlight. She lures them close then strikes them with a mallet on the head and robs them. To depict such scenes, Shuster used a pose nearly identical to that utilized in advertisements for Fritz Lang's classic 1945 noir *Scarlet Street,* a film about a prostitute who lures a meek, frustrated banker and amateur artist to his doom.

The noir imagery is also paramount in "Wanted: One Corpse!" (*Funnyman* #5). Louie the Louse pulls off a big bank heist but it is of no use because every cop in the city is looking for him. He decides that he'll have a plastic surgeon give his fingerprints to a corpse and the police will think that he is dead and stop pursuing him. He sends his moll, the blonde bombshell Lola, out to find a fall guy. Here male sexual infatuation is explicitly linked with death for when Lola's charms entice someone it also spells his demise.

The story registers male fears of the sexually aggressive female and of the destabilization of masculinity. In presenting himself as tough enough to join Louie's gang, Funnyman must pose as a tough guy, exposing masculinity itself as a performative masquerade. Masculinity is only a performance, an act rather than a biologically male trait. "Ya remember da Mahoucus Massacre?" he asks them in mock gangsterese, "I did dat!"; "Ya remember the Johnston Flood?" "My woik!" he boasts. However, the clown then undercuts the whole performance with a comic punch line: "Ya remember da Chicago Fire?" "I didn't do dat—some jealous competitor beat me to it!" Funnyman's attempt at bravado is painfully thin, more like an outdated vaudeville routine than an affirmation of toughness. Here macho masculinity has become so hyperbolic its credibility has become tenuous.

The deauthorization of the male is constructed in relationship to a perceived increase

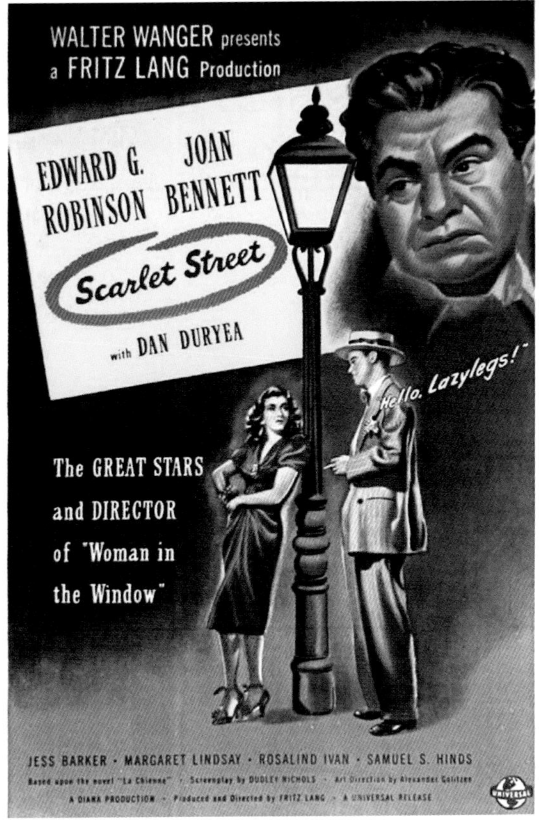

Movie poster from *Scarlet Street* (1945)

Panel from "The Kute Knockout! (Funnyman #2, 1948).

in female power and independence. In "Medieval Mirthquake" (*Funnyman* #4), the superhero is magically transported back in time to the Middle Ages. In a reprise of the King Arthur legend, Funnyman is threatened by Queen Hotcha, a spider woman who wants him to kill her husband, King Arterie, so that she can assume his throne. When Funnyman tells the king of the plot he thinks it a lie and makes the clown fight a duel with a huge giant who threatens to bash his skull. Women's new power and independence thus threaten the feminized male who does not possess the traditional values of masculine strength and toughness.

The Funnyman Comic Strip

From the first the *Funnyman* comic book had failed to generate sales. *Funnyman* #1 had suffered large returns and #6 left many issues unsold. However, Siegel and Shuster refused to give up on their new hero and decided to launch him as a newspaper comic strip in October 1948, several months after the cancellation of the *Funnyman* comic book. It is notable for marking significant changes in the their development of the character.

Newspaper comic strips differ from comic books in narrative structure and target audience. While comic book stories are meant to be consumed in a single reading, comic strip stories are often serialized over several months and thus may have complex narratives. They are also targeted more to adult readers and may have a more mature storyline than comic books. Eighty percent of American adults read newspaper comic strips; only a quarter of them read comic books. Comic strips were considered a more prestigious medium than children's comic books, the latter considered to be derivative and inferior to the former. Perhaps for these reasons, Shuster took more care with the artwork in Funnyman comic strips than he did in Funnyman comic books. He only loosely penciled the latter while his staff provided the finished artwork. As a result, the stories have a plethora of different styles and vary in quality. Shuster's style is more obvious in the Funnyman comic strip which evidences a uniform hand guiding it.

The *Funnyman* daily strip begins by recounting Funnyman's origin then launches into an adventure in which June joins the clown in fighting criminals. In the comic book stories June was confined to a marginal presence. Here we get a deeper view of her relationship with Larry Davis. There is more emphasis on June trying to entice Larry Davis away from his crime-fighter persona and into a romantic relationship with her. A glamour shot of June in a low-cut evening gown exemplifies the heightened emphasis on sexuality and romantic relationships in *Funnyman* as compared to Superman comics. Nevertheless, Funnyman violates the norms of heterosexual masculinity. "I get all dolled up in expectation of a romantic evening and wind up flying through the sky with a sherlocking Goofy Gargoyle!" she complains. The superhero is no longer a romantic but inaccessible figure but rather a geek a woman is loath to be seen with: "Strip off that clownish get-up, and revert to your everyday identity as comedian Larry Davis," June demands. "I want a date with a normal drip!" In contrast to Superman, the girlfriend would rather be with the alter ego than the costumed hero.

As in the Funnyman comic book, femmes fatales are prominent in the comic strip's gallery of villains, but with a crucial difference. The strip extends the role of Larry Davis, who is an incidental character in the comic book, to the lead in several stories. In one, for example, Davis becomes a romantic hero pitted against "the wealthiest woman in the world," Lola Leeds. Although Larry had an angular, slightly hawk-nosed face in comic books (and early comic strips), in this continuity Shuster draws him as a matinee idol who resembles Superman in some panels. "You have the profile of a Greek god," Lola tells him, and "a dynamic personality that would make women swoon from coast to coast."

Lola is a sexy, tyrannical woman, who tries to use both her charms and her power to bend Larry to her will. She owns a movie studio and orders the director to make Larry a star, forcing him to abandon June and his former friends—and his comic skills—to embark on a dubious career as a dramatic Hollywood lead. But when Larry catches her with another actor he realizes how fickle she is and goes back to being a nightclub comedian and June's boyfriend. As in the case of the noir femme fatale, female power is conflated with female dominance over the male and must be condemned.

Reggie Van Twerp

By early 1949 the syndicate began to see the writing on the wall and concluded that Funnyman was too off-putting. He began to appear less and less in the strip as it was taken over by secondary characters. The July 2, 1949 strip dropped Funnyman altogether and a new lead, Reggie Van Twerp, was introduced. This was a virtually unprecedented development in a comic strip feature. Siegel and Shuster had created Reggie in the mid-Thirties when they were still shopping Superman around to newspaper syndicates. Reggie was a young, wealthy naïf who is the victim of numerous schemers, usually women, who try to swindle money from him. The formula may have held some appeal for Depression audiences when Siegel first created Reggie, but also fit well with the misogynist anxieties of the postwar era.

Reggie is small, dark-haired, bespectacled, and timid—an exact replica of Siegel himself. But the character ultimately derives from famed author P.G. Wodehouse's Jeeves novels in which the wealthy ne'er-do-well Bertie Wooster is saved from various schemers by his omniscient valet, Jeeves. Indeed, in Wodehouse's first version of this series the young aristocrat is named Reggie. Siegel did not add a valet to his strip until the second adventure, but even from the first the Wodehouse influence is apparent.

Bertie was the victim of impetuous flirtations and short-lived engagements and tyrannized over by the formidable Aunt Agatha. In Reggie's first adventure his domineering Aunt Lucy forces him into agreeing to marry a "perfect stranger." Although Lucy thinks she is a "nice, quiet, old-fashioned girl," Clarice turns out to be a hellion. She drives 90 miles an hour in a high-speed car chase with a cop, and prefers jive music to a slow waltz. Flinging Reggie onto a tough's lap, Clarice tries to egg him into a fight with Reggie. The sequence culminates when she hits a visiting ambassador in the face with a pie when she finds his speech boring. Clarice is also overly sexually aggressive, chasing a reluctant Reggie up the draperies because she wants to kiss him. She epitomizes the stereotype of female excess, the unruly woman. In the story's conclusion she reveals that she is really Janice, "the Winston Wildcat," posing as her timid sister. In the postwar era images of women were split into good girls and bad girls, the sexual, aggressive woman and the passive, domestic woman, a rewriting of the virgin/whore dichotomy that had fascinated Victorians in the nineteenth century.

At the end of the adventure Aunt Lucy decides that Reggie should meet the real Clarice but he defiantly refuses and muses "Scheming women! If only there were some able chap around to give me a helping hand!." Enter Higgins, Jeeves' counterpart in the strip, who plays the role of the omniscient valet who is always able to get Reggie out of the hands of carpetbaggers and scheming women. The latter appears in the form of Goldie, a gold-digger as her name implies, who arrives, mother in tow, to spend time with Reggie and manipulate him into proposing. Like Aunt Lucy, Goldie's mother wants to arrange a marriage to a woman Reggie has never met. Higgins tries to oust the two women by starving them with too little food: "I'd like to wrap this plate around his head," Goldie thinks to herself. "But my day will come. When Reggie and I are married will I make him *miserable*!" Then Goldie tries to trick Reggie into proposing. She is a vampire whose very kiss spells Reggie's doom. She fakes a fainting spell and when Reggie approaches her he is irresistibly drawn to steal a kiss. "Great Scott, Higgins!" the butler tells the valet, "if that young Van Twerp kisses that vampire even once he is doomed!" This is no idle threat for she plans use the stolen kiss as a pretext for demanding that Reggie marry her. Higgins saves the day by telling Goldie and her mother a tall tale—that Reggie is a Jekyll and Hyde creature who turns into a "fiend...a monster...a beast" whose "hereditary taint" compels him to hunt down his victims—and the women flee in terror. Siegel conflates romantic comedy with the horror film, making Reggie into a werewolf for a laugh. But the mixing of genres shows how he was unable to shake his past and write a straight romantic comedy. The hysteria surrounding sexual/romantic involvement with women and the fear of the ensuing emasculation/destruction surrounding this encounter reflects the sexual crisis of the period in which men were both attracted to and repelled by women, when lovers could be seen as threats to a man's job—and his identity.

Mothers during this period also came in for condemnation. In 1942 Phillip Wylie's *Generation of Vipers* was published and became an immediate bestseller. Wylie attacked "Momism"—the rule of the self-righteous, hypocritical, sexually repressed middle-aged woman. Having lost her household functions, mom got men to worship her and spend money on her instead. America, claimed Wylie, was "a matriarchy in fact if not in declaration" in which "the women of America raped the men." [41] Mom dominated not only her husband but also encouraged her son to be dependent on her, claimed Wylie. We can see vestiges of the fear of Momism in Siegel's characterization of the domineering Aunt Lucy (a mother surrogate) and Goldie's gold-digging mother.

The disparagement of moms was paralleled by the emergence of negative stereotypes of the Jewish mother in the postwar era. [42] Both Jewish and Gentile mothers were condemned for smothering their sons and failing to raise them into proper men. However, the Jewish stereotype derived from more specific anxieties surrounding issues of Jewish assimilation and identity. Jewish men confronted competing pressures: to achieve success and acceptance in the larger society while maintaining their ethnic and religious origins within the family. Jewish women came to represent the conflicts inherent in these tasks. Mothers demanded that their male offspring achieve affluence and success yet set strict limits to male assimilation by urging them to resist romantic involvement with Gentile women. This is one of the reasons for the stereotype of Jewish mothers as domineering and overbearing. Siegel references this stereotype in his depiction of Aunt Lucy and Goldie's mother attempting to decide whom Reggie should marry

The fears of scheming women fleecing newly minted millionaires not only embodied anxieties arising from gender and ethnic conflicts, but also encoded Siegel's feelings about his bitter and costly divorce from his wife Bela in 1948. Bela filed for divorce in July, 1948.

The decree was granted in October, the same month the *Funnyman* strip first appeared. In a 2007 letter Joanne Siegel, Jerry's second wife, described the toll which the divorce took on him: "After a hostile and expensive divorce, Jerry was without a home or car and had very little money left. He was not working on Superman any longer and his new comic book, *Funnyman*, became a flop just months later. This left him flat broke."[43] Goldie's scheming and desire to make Reggie miserable when they are wed reveals a cynicism about marriage that was absent from Siegel's earlier work. Siegel's portrayal of domineering matriarchs had roots in his own family situation. Siegel's mother was the matriarch of the Siegel family, especially after his father died in the early Thirties. Jerry lived alone with her for several years after his brother and sisters moved out. Sarah was very disapproving of his marriage to Bela, as were Jerry's aunts. As a result, Siegel became estranged from his family after the marriage and rarely saw family members.

Shuster's drawings of *Funnyman*'s femmes fatales are similarly autobiographical. They are tall, blonde, and bosomy like the showgirls and models that he idealized. Five-foot-two and Jewish, Shuster would only date tall women. "He loved shiksas," comments Jean Shuster Peavy, "they were always tall and slender blondes like his dream girl Lana Turner."[44] Turner's form-fitting attire gave her the nickname of "the sweater girl" in the 1940s. The shiksa goddess was an object of fascination for the Jewish nebbish because it involved the taboo of having a romance with a Gentile. The winning of a tall woman must have also given a feeling of masculine power and conquest to a short man. Shuster remained enamored of this ideal even in his senior years and at 62 married a tall, bosomy Las Vegas showgirl, a marriage that lasted only a year.

End Game

The Funnyman Sunday tales bear a closer resemblance to those in the comic book and feature more of the clown battling criminals than the dailies. This is because Sunday strip adventures are more geared toward a family audience than the dailies, and presume a readership of both children and adults. The more frequent appearances of Funnyman in the Sundays enabled Siegel to vent some of his anger and frustration about the injustice of his failed lawsuit with National and loss of rights to Superman. In a tale beginning November 21, 1948, Larry Davis is a music publisher and has received a letter from a lawyer that his client, Winston Lightfingers of Gypsum Mine, Inc. owns the rights to the song "Piddle-Paddle Glook," and that he's publishing it illegally. Jerkimer, the writer of the song, had been approached by Lightfingers at a nightclub where he offered the author a contract he'll "never forget." When Jerkimer asked for an advance the shyster laughed and told him to "reread that contract's small print!!!" and that he will get nothing. A hidden clause stated that he will publish the song "only if he is out of his mind" and declared that the writer is a victim of a "practical joke." Siegel portrays the publisher as a villain satirizing the way shysters legally swindle authors through using legal mumbo jumbo, a clear reference to National's purchase of the copyright to Superman for $130.

When Jerkimer takes Lightfingers to court the shyster's attorney is able to obtain a favorable ruling from the magistrate, Judge Gleason, through fraud. Lightfingers has been committed to a mental hospital where he feigns mental incompetence, thereby fulfilling the terms of the contract. He plans to have himself declared miraculously cured and then claim the profits for the song. The story's conflicts are resolved in true superhero fashion: Funnyman saves the day by broadcasting Lightfinger's confession from the hospital that the illness was a scam. Hearing the news Judge Gleason has the crooks arrested and Larry Davis's royalties restored. Although Siegel and Shuster might have wished for such a utopian resolution, in real life justice would be deferred and it would take 30 years for them to receive vindication.

Although morally valid, this story was heavy-handed and too creaky to sustain a compelling narrative. Indeed, the Funnyman comic strips revealed the writer's limitations when he wrote scripts for characters other than Superman. In an attempt to create new stories Siegel began recycling material from other characters. In a 1948 daily adventure he gives Funnyman a juvenile sidekick named Funnyboy, aping Batman and Robin. The Batman influence was also evident in the numerous gadgets Funnyman used to outwit criminals and most blatantly in Siegel's reference to Funnyman's home as "Funnymanor," a swipe from Wayne Manor, Bruce Wayne's estate in *Batman*. Mostly, however, Siegel stole from himself, endlessly regurgitating plots and characters that harkened back to his early days as a struggling fan writer. In the last Reggie Van Twerp daily strip adventure, for example, Reggie is victimized by a mad scientist who promises to invent a serum that will transform him into a "super brain."[45] The plot recycles Siegel's first superman story, "Reign of the Superman," in which a mad scientist injects a man from the breadline with a serum that transforms him into a telepathic superman. Although Siegel twists the tale to comic uses, it suggests that he was running out of fresh ideas and having trouble working in a format he was unaccustomed to. Siegel was also losing the idealism that had made Superman such a success. While the Man of Steel was a champion of the underdog and the common man in his early adventures, in this tale the hoi polloi are mob-like scavengers. Doc Fizz's relatives try to live rent-free off Reggie and their drunken manners bring him social disgrace.

As in many of these stories there is an autobiographical element. Siegel's parents criticized him for dreaming of becoming a famous comics creator and for not taking a job in his father's haberdashery store. Often unemployed, Siegel lived at home with his mother after his father's death and may have felt some guilt about not being a breadwinner, reflected in the condemnation of Fizz's freeloading relatives living rent-free with Reggie.

Funnyman was Siegel and Shuster's last collaboration. An almost 20-year business and friendship ended with the two partners seeking their fortunes separately. Siegel went on to work sporadically but fairly regularly in the comic book industry, becoming editor of the Ziff-Davis line of comics between 1950 and 1953. He would return to work on Superman as an anonymous writer working for page rates between 1959 and 1966. Siegel ended up so anguished over losing Superman that he could no longer write comics and worked in anonymity as a $7,000-a-year file clerk in Los Angeles.

Shuster fared even worse. His eyesight, already bad when he was working for National, steadily deteriorated after the trial. Because of his poor vision he and Siegel would never work together again. By the 1950s, Shuster had become nearly blind in one eye. He was still able to pencil a few horror and crime comics, but his pencil work was so indistinct that the art is not recognizably his. Shuster also had a short-lived career drawing S&M illustrations for men's magazines, indulging his penchant for sexy women. These illustrations show that, despite his vision problems, Shuster could still draw well. But he was ashamed to be working in this venue, and never signed his name to his art. For twenty-five years he lived in near-poverty with his brother Frank in New York, nostalgically conjuring up his faded days of glory.

Since 1948, Siegel's and Shuster's names had been stricken from Superman comics and they had received no royalties from the character. A legal settlement in 1975 restored their byline and gave them a modest pension. Shuster died in 1992 and his partner four years later. In 2008 Siegel's heirs recaptured some of the rights to Superman, and Shuster's estate is in line to share in the reclamation of their original rights to the character. It is a fitting vindication for a duo that created the ultimate symbol of "Truth, Justice, and the American Way."

Notes

1 *Cobblestone*, December 1975.

2 See Danny Fingeroth, *Disguised as Clark Kent: Jews, Comics, and the Creation of the Superhero*, (New York: Continuum, 2007) and Simcha Weinstein, *Up, Up, and Oy Vey! How Jewish History, Culture, and Values Shaped the Comic Book Superhero*, (Baltimore, Maryland: Leviathan Press, 2006).

3 Thomas Andrae interview with Jean Shuster Peavy, June 8, 2009.

4 *Alter Ego* Vol. 3, #10 (September, 2001).

5 Thomas Andrae, Interview with Jerry Siegel and Joe Shuster, Feb. 25, 1981.

6 *The Glenville Torch* May 7, 1931.

7 Thomas Andrae, interview with Jean Shuster Peavy, July 12, 2008.

8 This is only partially true: Shuster ran track, was on the tumbling team, and was a bodybuilder while in high school.

9 Paula Hyman, *Gender and Assimilation in Modern Jewish History: The Roles and Representation of Women*, (Seattle: University of Washington Press, 1995), 134.

10 Maurice Berger, "The Mouse That Never Roars: Jewish Masculinity on American Television," in Norman Kleeblatt, *Too Jewish: Challenging Traditional Identity* (New Brunswick: Rutgers University Press, 1996).

11 Paul Breines, *Tough Jews: Political Fantasies and the Moral Dilemma of American Jewry* (New York: Basic Books, 1990), 44.

12 *Tough Jews*, 45.

13 *Tough Jews*, 127.

14 Samson, a Jewish strongman, is one exception. Siegel refers to him in describing his creation of Superman, and Shuster drew a Sampson-like Superman tearing down columns of a building on the cover of *Superman* #4 (Spring, 1940) and utilized this image of Samson in a story in *Superman* #2 (1939).

15 John Kobler, "Up, Up and Awa-a-y! The Rise of Superman, Inc.," *Saturday Evening Post*, June 21, 1941, 98.

16 Kenneth Dutton, *The Perfectible Body: The Western Ideal of Male Physical Development*, (New York: Continuum, 1995), 199.

17 Jules Feiffer, "The Minsk Theory of Krypton: Jerry Siegel (1914-1996)," *New York Times Magazine*, December 29, 1996, 14–15.

18 Ibid.

19 Jerry Siegel, press release, October 1975.

20 An example of the latter is Kent's visit to the country of Dukalia for the Sports Festival, an allusion to the 1936 Berlin Olympics in which Hitler vainly boasted about the superiority of the Aryan race only to have Germans defeated by the African-American Jesse Owens (*Superman* #10, 1941)

21 See *Disguised as Clark Kent*, 39–50 and *Up, Up, and Oy Vey*, 19–32.

22 Jerry Siegel, *The Creation of a Superhero*, unpublished manuscript, 1976, 82. Jor-l's name was later changed to Jor-El.

23 Aldo Regaldo, "Modernity, Race, and the American Superhero" in Jeff Mclaughlin (ed.), *Comics as Philosophy*, (Jackson: University Press of Mississippi, 2005).

24 Richard Alba and Victor Nee, *Remaking the American Mainstream: Assimilation and Contemporary Immigration*, (Cambridge: Harvard University Press, 2003), 115–116.

25 Klaus Theweleit, *Male Fantasies*, 2 vols. (Minneapolis: University of Minnesota Press, 1977).

26 Andrae, interview with Jerry Siegel and Joe Shuster, 1981.

27 Ibid.

28 Ibid.

29 See Jerry Siegel, "Superman's Return to Krypton," *Superman* #141 (November 1960). Siegel's stories during this period reveal a tragic side to Superman: In this tale the Man of Steel travels to the past before Krypton was destroyed and tries vainly to save his parents and his new love, Lyla Lerrol, a Kryptonian actress, from being destroyed with the planet.

30 Jerry Siegel, "The Death of Superman," *Superman* #149, October 1961.

31 Siegel wrote the story in October 1940.

32 Thomas Andrae, *Creators of the Superheroes* (Philadelphia: Hermes Press, 2010).

33 Gary Engle, "What Makes Superman So Darned American?" in Denis Dooley and Gary Engel (eds.), *Superman at Fifty! The Persistence of a Legend* (New York: Collier, 1988).

34 "The Downfall of Noodnik Nogoodnik" *Funnyman* # 5 (July, 1948).

35 Martin Gottfried, *The Many Lives of Danny Kaye* (New York: Simon and Shuster, 1994), 85.

36 Gottfried disputes Kaye's homosexuality although other biographers disagree. See *The Many Lives of Danny Kaye*, 194–195.

37 Jean-Paul Gabrillet, *Of Comics and Men: A Cultural History of American Comic Books* (Jackson: University Press of Mississippi, 2010), 34.

38 *Creation of a Superhero*, 78.

39 See Thomas Andrae, "From Menace to Messiah: The Prehistory of the Superman in Science Fiction Literature," *Discourse: Berkeley Journal for Theoretical Studies in Media and Culture* #2 (Summer, 1980).

40 *Of Comics and Men: A Cultural History of American Comic Books*, 30.

41 Philip Wylie, *Generation of Vipers* (New York: Pocket Books, 1942), 184–196. Wylie's science fiction novel *Gladiator* (1930) has also been credited as one of the inspirations for Siegel's creation of Superman.

42 *Gender and Assimilation in Modern Jewish History*, 158–160.

43 Joanne Siegel, letter to the Superman Homepage, p://www.supermanhomepage.com/comics.php.

44 Thomas Andrae, interview with Jean Shuster Peavy, March 17, 2009.

45 Siegel also recycled the figure of a mental superman in another *Funnyman* daily strip adventure, "Funnyman vs. Bighead" (1948).

FUNNYMAN
COMIC BOOK STORIES

"The Kute Knockout!" (*Funnyman #2* March 1948)

SHORTLY AFTER TORGO REVIVES.
WHAT IS SHE? A BOOBY TRAP?
EXACTLY. "THE KUTE KNOCKOUT," A ROBOT GIRL, SERVES AS A FEMININE LURE FOR PROSPECTIVE VICTIMS.
WE PLACE HER ON A DARK STREET. WHEN A VICTIM APPROACHES, SHE DROPS THE HANKY. HE GALLANTLY BENDS TO LIFT IT, THEN--WHANGO! --HE GETS BOPPED WITH THE MALLET! IT'S ALL DONE WITH PHOTO-ELECTRIC CELLS!
AN' THEN-- HO! HO! HO!-- WE CLEANS OUT HIS POCKETS! DOC--YA DONE IT AGIN!!!
NIGHTFALL
HOOT MON! WHAT AN EYE-DAZZLER... AND SHE'S DROPPED HER HANKY! ROMANCE, HERE I COME!
THUD!
YAK, YAK! HOW DID WE DO, TORGO?
GREAT! HE WAS LOADED WITH TH' CRINKLY GREEN STUFF!
A BEAUTEOUS CHICK WHO SLUGS 'EM AND ROBS 'EM! HM-MM! WONDER IF I COULD NAB HER... AS FUNNYMAN!?
STAR
CITY PLAGUED BY RASH OF GIRL-LURE ROBBERIES
WOULD-BE ROMEOS ROBBED
CRIME-GAL KONKS VICTI
FOR THE INFO OF NEW READERS NOT YET HEP TO THE SITUATION, ACE COMEDIAN LARRY DAVIS IS NONE OTHER THAN COMIC CRIMEBUSTER ...FUNNYMAN!
2

THAT EVENING.
'TWAS IN THIS VERY NEIGHBORHOOD THAT THE DARK DEEDS WERE DONE! MAYHAPS, IF I SCOUT ABOUT...

THAT WINSOME MISS OVER YONDER SOMEWHAT RESEMBLES THE GAL IN THE NEWSPAPER ACCOUNTS.

--AND SHE'S DROPPED HER HANDKERCHIEF... JUST LIKE IT SAID IN TH' NEWSPAPER YARNS...

ALLOW ME, MADAME!
WHAT'S THIS? FUNNYMAN DELIBERATELY STICKING HIS ADDLEPATED CRANIUM INTO THE WAY OF DISASTER--???

IT'S THAT ACCURSED SCREWBALL SLEUTH! FUNNYMAN! BUT "THE KUTE KNOCKOUT" WILL TAKE GOOD CARE OF HIM!
HAW! HAW! SHE SHORE WILL!
3

OH-OH! HERE IT COMES! OUT OF THE ROBOT-GIRL FLASHES A HUGE MALLET TOWARD THE SKULL OF THE UNSUSPECTING (?) VICTIM!
GOOD THING I'M NOT THE SUSPICIOUS TYPE! OTHERWISE I'D HAVE PLENTY OF CAUSE TO WORRY!

...AND CONNECTS!
SM-MACK!
AH! GOT IT!
BUT--WONDERS OF WONDERS!--THE TREMENDOUS BLOW APPARENTLY HAS NO EFFECT ON THE COURAGEOUS CLOWN!
SO-LONG! GOODBYE! AND OTHER SUCH SALUTATIONS OF FAREWELL!
INCREDIBLE! THAT BLOW SHOULD HAVE SPLIT HIS SKULL--YET HE ACTS LIKE HE'D ONLY GOTTEN A SCALP MASSAGE!
SOMETHIN' MUSTA GONE WRONG WID DA "KUTE KNOCKOUT"'S MECHANISM, DOC.
I'LL INVESTIGATE!
CR-RACK!
AGH!
HEY!
I DON'T GET IT! THAT MALLET BLOW DIDN'T BOTHER FUNNYMAN ONE BIT-- YET IT KNOCKED DOC FOR A LOOP
HO! HO!- CONFUSIN', WOT?
4

YA PUNY SQUIRT! I'LL TEAR YA LIMB FROM LIMB!
METHINKS YOU'RE NOTHIN' BUT...
WHOOSH!
...A BIG BAG OF WIND!
LATER
--AND SO YOU SEE, OFFICER, DOC GIMMICK AND HIS HIRELING PERPETRATED THE GIRL-LURE CRIMES WITH A ROBOT THAT HAD A MALLET CUNNINGLY CONCEALED WITHIN IT.
AMAZING! BUT WHY DID THE MALLET FAIL TO KNOCK YOU OUT??
BECAUSE I WAS ADEQUATELY PREPARED FOR THE FRAY! BEHOLD-- A METAL SKULL-CAP ADORNED WITH CAMOUFLAGING FAKE HAIR!
IMAGINE THAT!!
NEXT DAY.
LARRY! THAT GIRL DROPPED HER HANDKERCHIEF! THE LEAST YOU COULD HAVE DONE WAS PICK IT UP!
NOT ME, JUNE!
I LEFT MY METAL SKULL-CAP HOME!
METAL SKULL-CAP? LARRY, SOMETIMES I THINK YOU'RE NOT "ALL THERE"! ("-'SOMETIMES,' DID I SAY??-")
5
THE END

FUNNYMAN

by JERRY SIEGEL and JOE SHUSTER

HOLY HOKY! A CELESTIAL HOT-FOOT!!

THE FIGHTING FOOL

OH YOU KID!

ZOWIE!

OUT FOR AN EVENING'S ADVENTURE-SOME CRUISE IN THE *JET-JALLOPY, FUNNYMAN*—WHO IN HIS OTHER GUISE IS LARRY DAVIS, TOP COMEDIAN-IS SUDDENLY CAUGHT IN THE FIERCE GRIP OF A GREAT STORM. SUDDENLY, A BLINDING BURST OF LIGHTNING CRASHES INTO THE *FLYIN' FLIVVER*, LAUNCHING OUR *DAFFY DAREDEVIL* INTO HIS UNEXPECTED ROLE AS.... "THE *MEDIEVAL MIRTHQUAKE*"

DOWN THRU THE HEAVENS, TO THE ACCOMPANIMENT OF DEAFENING THUNDER, WHIRLS THE STRICKEN VEHICLE.

BROAD DAYLIGHT! MAYBE THAT BOLT OF LIGHTNING KNOCKED THE REMAINING HALF OF A WIT OUTO MY SKULL!

23 SKIDOO

1

"The Medieval Mirthquake" (*Funnyman* #4 May 1948)

NOW I KNOW I'M SEEIN' THINGS!
MONSTER FROM THE SKIES -- I SHALL SLAY THEE EVEN AS I SLEW A DRAGON ONLY YESTERDAY!

IMAGINARY VISION OR NOT, FUNNYMAN IS TAKING NO CHANCES. AT A TOUCH OF A BUTTON, AN ELECTRICALLY CHARGED DEFENCE-GADGET FLIPS INTO VIEW.
YII-IIII! I'M BEWITCHED
SHOCKING, WOT?

MERCY! OH ALL POWERFUL MAGICIAN!
YA WORK FOR A CIRCUS, MAC -- OR ARE YA TRAIPSIN' TO A MASQUERADE-BALL?
OBVIOUSLY, YOU HAIL FROM A FOREIGN CLIME, FOR EVEN THE LOWEST LACKEY WOULD RECOGNIZE ME AS SIR LUNCHALOT OF THE COURT OF KING ARTERY!
?

-SOMEHOW THAT LIGHTNING-BOLT TRANSPORTED BOTH TH' JET JALLOPY AN'ME BACK TA MEDIEVAL DAYS!
2

(SOB)-MAROONED IN TH' PAST! ..NEVER (SOB!) TA SEE JUNE'S SWEET FACE AGAIN...OR (SOB!) TH' HOMELY PUSS O' SGT. HARRIGAN...OR HOT DOGS, OR ICE CREAM, OR BASE-BALL GAMES... (SOB!!!)...
YOU DO NOT APPEAR TOO BAD A LOT. COME! I WILL TAKE YOU TO KING ARTERY!

BEHOLD! THE DOMAIN OF KING ARTERY!
GEE! JUS' LIKE IN TH' PITCHER-BOOKS!
23 SKIDOO

KNAVES! LOWER THE DRAWBRIDGE FOR SIR LUNCHALOT AND HIS GUEST!
AND ADMIT THAT FEARFUL CREATURE? NEVER!!

HO! HO!--IT WON'T BE TH' FIRST TIME I EVER CRASHED TH' GATE!
YOU ARE INDEED A WONDROUS WIZARD!
23 SKIDOO
TWO SCHEMING PAIRS OF EYES OBSERVE THE UNIQUE ENTRY.
ZOUNDS! AN INTERLOPER!
AND A RIVAL SORCERER, AT THAT! TEE-HEE! YOU FEAR HE MAY PROVE A RIVAL FOR THE KING'S FAVOR, EH, SCHMERLIN??

HIS WICKED LITTLE EYES SPARKLING MISCHEVIOUSLY, ZANIE, THE KING'S JESTER, SCAMPERS TO THE SUITE OF HIS SECRET MASTER, SCHEMING QUEEN HOTCHA.
YOUR HUMBLE SERVANT BRINGS STRANGE AND EXCITING NEWS, OH BEAUTEOUS QUEEN! A STRANGER--A WORKER OF MARVELS--HAS ENTERED THE CASTLE!
FETCH MY MOST EXOTIC PERFUMES... ("-MAYHAPS THIS NEW-COMER CAN MATERIALIZE MY AMBITION TO DESTROY KING ARTERY AND RULE---ALONE!-")
3

SOON AFTER, FUNNYMAN IS RECEIVED IN A MANNER BEFITTING A VISITING MAGICIAN.
WELCOME TO MY KINGDOM. WOULDST THOU CARE TO WITNESS SCHMERLIN, THE COURT MAGICIAN, DEMONSTRATE HIS ARTS?
WHY NOT?
HM-MPH!

SCHMERLIN PERFORMS SEVERAL SIMPLE TRICKS.
BEHOLD! WATER INTO BLOOD!
PHOOIE! ARE YOU CORNY! NO WONDER VAUDEVILLE IS DEAD!
IF THE HONORED GUEST FEELS HE CAN DO BETTER, HE IS WELCOME TO TRY!

THE PRINCE OF PRANKSTERS ACCEPTS THE CHALLENGE. HE WHIPS AN ALARM-CLOCK FROM HIS FLOPPY JEANS.
IT LITERALLY TELLS TIME!
HE IS INDEED A MIRACLE MAN!
RRR-RR-RR

FUNNYMAN DASHES OFF TO THE JET-JALLOPY AND RETURNS WITH AN EVEN GREATER SENSATION.
A GIFT FROM ME TO YOU, YOUR MAJESTY!
DELIGHTFUL!

HOWZIS FER A YOK-GETTER? A RABBIT OUTA SCHMERLIN'S BONNET!
BY MY ANCESTORS, YOU ARE THE GREATEST WIZARD OF THEM ALL! WOULD THAT YOU WERE MY COURT MAGICIAN
LOUT!

ZANIE! OUR GUEST HAS OFFERED MORE THAN HIS SHARE OF ENTERTAINMENT. TITILLATE HIM WITH SOME TOMFOOLERY!
TEE-HEE! AS YOU COMMAND, MOST MIGHTY OF ALL MONARCHS!
YOU'LL BE ENTRANCED! ZANIE IS THE MOST COMICAL JESTER IN ALL THE KINGDOMS! (CHUCKLE)
YEAH? ODD HE'S NEVER MADE TH' TOP HOOPER RATINGS!
4

DELIBERATELY, ZANIE SPRINTS ACROSS THE THRONE ROOM AT TOP SPEED, THEN...
HAA- HAA-AA!
("-??... IT SEEMS THAT THE LAUGHTER OF THIS PERIOD IS DEPENDENT ON CRUELTY AND VIO- LENCE-")
CLUNK!

NEXT, THE JESTER PURSUES A CRIPPLED LAD ABOUT THE ROOM, WHACKING HIM WITH A BLADDER.
HYAK! HYAW- HAWW-WWW!
THE BULLY!

UGH-HH!
LAUGH THAT OFF!
EVERYBODY WANTS TO GET INTO THE ACT!
A MINOR- LEAGUE DURANTE, HAH?

POP-FLY!
5

A TOSS TO HOME- PLATE! YOU'RE OUT!
NOT ONLY IS THE STRANGER A MAGICIAN--BUT-- A COMEDIAN!

SPUTTERING WITH FURY, FUNNYMAN'S FOE HOISTS A WATER-BAG ALOFT, AND CHARGES...
WE'LL SEE WHO IS REALLY THE FOOL!
MAY I?
YOU MAY!
A LITTLE DAMP BEHIND THE EARS, AREN'T YOU??
(GASP!) (SPLUTTER)
LATER
I HATE HIM! OH, HOW I HATE HIM!!
YOU'LL HAVE YOUR VENGEANCE, MY FAITHFUL FOOL, AFTER YOU LURE HIM INTO MY TOILS!
AND SO--LATER STILL...
THIS IS THE STRANGER'S CHAMBER. IF THE RED-NOSED ONE OBEYS THIS NOTE'S INSTRUCTIONS....TEE-HEE-HEE-EE...HE'S DOOMED!
THIS NOTE--WRIT IN A FEMININE HAND--IMPLORES ME TO FOLLOW THE BEAN-TRAIL...FOR THE SAKE OF A LOVELY LADY!--I DOOED IT!!
6
G-G-GULP!!

--ARE YOU **SURE** THIS ISN'T A CASE OF MISTAKEN IDENTITY, MADAME QUEEN?

THERE'S NO MISTAKE! WE WERE MEANT FOR EACH OTHER! BUT THE KING STANDS IN THE WAY OF OUR GREAT LOVE--THEREFORE, BELOVED, YOU MUST **KILL** HIM WITH YOUR MYSTIC POWERS!

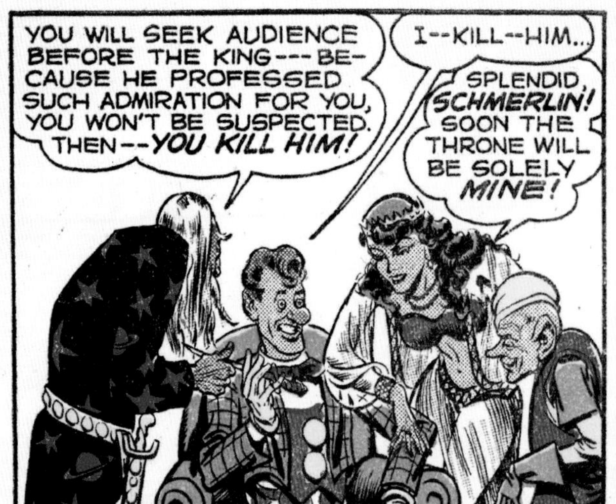
YOU WILL SEEK AUDIENCE BEFORE THE KING--- BECAUSE HE PROFESSED SUCH ADMIRATION FOR YOU, YOU WON'T BE SUSPECTED. THEN--YOU KILL HIM!
I--KILL--HIM...
SPLENDID, SCHMERLIN! SOON THE THRONE WILL BE SOLELY MINE!

BUT, AFTER THE SLAPHAPPY SLUGGER LEAVES THE PLOTTERS' PRESENCE...
WHEW! GOOD THING I SPILLED OUT HALF THAT DRUGGED DRINK, UNNOTICED BY THE QUEEN. I HAD JUST ENOUGH WILL-POWER TO SUCCESSFULLY RESIST SCHMERLIN'S AUTO-SUGGESTION!

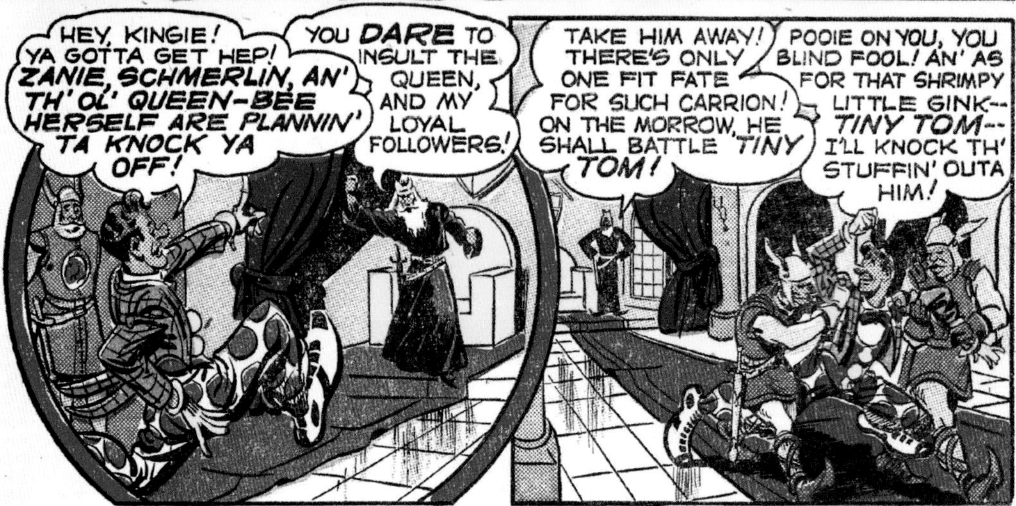
HEY, KINGIE! YA GOTTA GET HEP! ZANIE, SCHMERLIN, AN' TH' OL' QUEEN-BEE HERSELF ARE PLANNIN' TA KNOCK YA OFF!
YOU DARE TO INSULT THE QUEEN, AND MY LOYAL FOLLOWERS!
TAKE HIM AWAY! THERE'S ONLY ONE FIT FATE FOR SUCH CARRION! ON THE MORROW, HE SHALL BATTLE TINY TOM!
POOIE ON YOU, YOU BLIND FOOL! AN' AS FOR THAT SHRIMPY LITTLE GINK--TINY TOM--I'LL KNOCK TH' STUFFIN' OUTA HIM!

COMES THE DAWN
YIPE!--IS TH-THAT (ULP!)--TINY TOM?
8

(PS-ST! TINY TOM HAS BEEN INFORMED THAT IF HIS MACE SHOULD ACCIDENTLY KILL THE KING, HE WILL BE FREED.)
(EXCELLENT! BUT, NATURALLY, WE WON'T KEEP OUR WORD!)
(SIGH) I RATHER LIKED THE STRANGER. HOW UNFORTUNATE HE TURNED OUT TO BE A BLACK VILLAIN.
TINY TOM'S MANACLES ARE REMOVED. HE IS ARMED WITH GIANT MACE AND AXE. THEN--A GONG CLANGS--HERALDS TOOT TRUMPETS ...AND THE MAIN EVENT IS ON!
HAWWW-HAWWW-HAWWW!!!
WOTSA BIG JOKE?
HO! HO! HEE! HO!!
AAWRK!
HO! HO! HEE! HO!!
KICKIE!
9

HOLY HOKEY!!
TO HECK WITH THIS STEEL STRAIGHT-JACKET! I'LL SHED IT AND FIGHT LIKE A MAN--STILL BETTER, FIGHT LIKE FUNNYMAN!!
THAT WAS TOO CLOSE FOR COMFORT!
WHAM!
AGILEY, THE FIGHTING FOOL ELUDES HIS BROBDINGNAGIAN OPPONENT'S STAMPING FEET...
STRATEGY... THAS WOT TH' SITUATION CALLS FER!
10

UP A TALL POLE HE CLAMBERS WITH ANTHROPOID SKILL.
YOU MEAN, YOU'LL TRY!
I GOING TO SWAT YOU LIKE FLY!
("THIS CALLS FOR QUICK ACTION-- AND A SWIFTER GETAWAY!-")
SOON, YOU'LL GO BOOM!
YEEEOOOWWW!!!
GOTTA GO!
BL-LAM
AS FUNNYMAN STRIKES EARTH, HE RELEASES THE SPRINGS IN THE SOLES OF HIS SHOES, AND THE RE-COIL SENDS HIM HURTLING UPWARD AGAIN.
COME BACK!
BOING
11

HE MAY BE A KNAVE -- BUT HE HAS COURAGE....AND WHAT A WIZARD HE IS!!
"-ENJOY YOUR LAST LIVING MOMENTS, MY DEAR--FOR YOU HAVEN'T MUCH LONGER TO LIVE!-"
TAKE A WHIFF O' LAUGHING-GAS... COURTESY O'TH FUNNYGUN!
THE COLOSSAL CREATURE COUGHS-- RUBS ITS WATERING EYES UNCOMPREHENDINGLY--THEN... LAUGHS AND LAUGHS, AND LAUGHS!!!
HAAA-AAA-AAA HO-HO-HO-HEEE-HEEE-HEEE! HAWW-HAAA-HAA-HAWWW-HAAA-HAWW- (COUGH!) HYAAAH-AAH.... (COUGH!)...
STILL CACKLING, BUT HALF-BLINDED, THE MONSTER CONTINUES ITS ATTEMPT TO DESTROY THE VEXING FOE!
HEE-EEE-HEE-EEE-HAAA-AA AHH-..!
CAN'T LET THIS GO ON INDEFINITELY! I'LL HAVE TO APPLY THE FINISHING TOUCH!
AN' THIS IS TH' LI'L GIMMICK THAT'LL DO TH' TRICK!
12

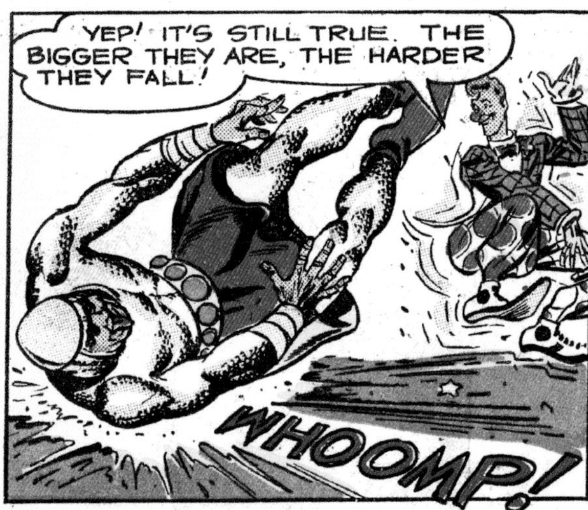

THE MIGHTY FALL HAS STUNNED *TINY TOM*. BUT REALIZING HE IS RAPIDLY SINKING INTO UNCONSCIOUSNESS, AND RECALLING HIS PROMISE-- HE PAINFULLY FORCES HIMSELF SLIGHTLY UPWARD, AND...

FUNNYMAN'S BULLET PIERCES A ROPE SUSPENDING AN ORNAMENTAL SHIELD A FEW FEET BEFORE AND ABOVE KING ARTERY'S HEAD.
CLANG
QUICK-- WHILE THE KING'S GUARDS ARE DISTRACTED. KILL HIM! THE ASSASSIN WILL RECEIVE ONE-FOURTH OF THE KINGDOM!
HE'S MINE!
NO-- MINE!!!
BUT HELP IS ON THE WAY!
HOO-HA!!
THE MAGNIFICENT STRANGER!
RIGHT, YOUR HIGHNESS!
TO THINK I HAD YOU SLATED FOR EXTINCTION-- WHEN YOUR SINCERE WARNING WAS ABSOLUTELY TRUE CAN YOU FORGIVE ME?
AW! IT WAS NUTTIN'!
AS A SYMBOL OF MY GRATITUDE, I AWARD YOU THIS CLOAK, WHICH HAS BEEN IN MY FAMILY FOR CENTURIES. AND I REQUEST YOU TO ACCEPT THE OFFICE OF KING'S COUNSELLOR!
GEE! THIS CALLS FOR A CELEBR-ATION!
14

AMAZING! YOU WHISTLE-AND YOUR VEHICLE COMES IN RESPONSE!
TWE-E-E-E
WATCH! YOU'LL SEE TH' GREATEST SKY-SHOW OF 'EM ALL! AN' I'LL SPORT YOUR CLOAK, IN YOUR HONOR!
THRU MEDIEVAL SKIES LOOPS AND CAVORTS A JET-PROPELLED VEHICLE. BUT SUDDENLY--IN THE MIDST OF A SWOOPING CURVE.....
YIPE! - W-WE'RE DISAPPEARIN'!!
23 SKIDOO
POW
HE'S VANISHED! THE WIZARD IS --GONE!!
I HAVE A FEELING WE'LL NEVER SEE HIM AGAIN. FRANKLY, SIR LUNCHALOT-- I'LL MISS HIM!
NEXT INSTANT--FUNNYMAN AND JET-JALLOPY MATERIALIZE IN THE DARK OF NIGHT.
WHEE!-THE TIME-TRAVELLING EFFECTS WORE OFF!..BUT WAIT! ACCORDING TO THE INSTRUMENTS, IT'S ONLY A BRIEF SECOND SINCE THE LIGHTNING STRUCK!
(SIGH!) KNIGHTS--OGRES--MEDIEVAL TIMES...!-SO IT WAS JUST A FIGMENT OF MY IMAGINATION! BUT IT SEEMED SO REAL!
15
POW
THE END

FUNNYMAN

by JERRY SIEGEL and JOE SHUSTER

HEY! LEGGO O' THAT LOOT! – Signed, Funnyman

NUTS TO YOU, FUNNYMAN! – Signed, Leapin' Lena

AS THO FUNNYMAN HASN'T TROUBLES ENOUGH, HE HAD TO GO AND MEET UP WITH THAT LARCENOUS LADY KNOWN AS... "LEAPIN' LENA"!

"Leapin' Lena" (Funnyman #4 May 1948)

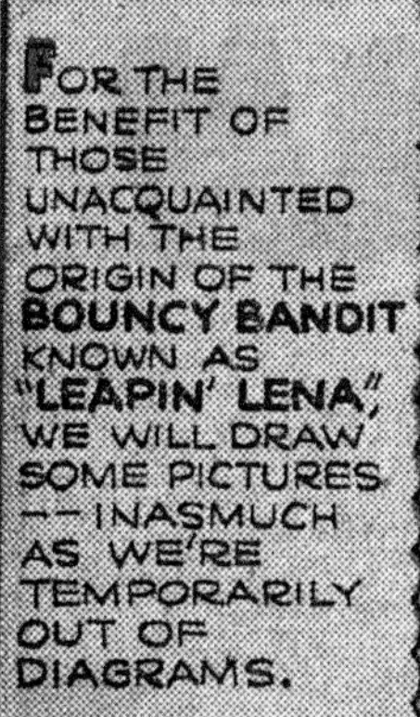
FOR THE BENEFIT OF THOSE UNACQUAINTED WITH THE ORIGIN OF THE BOUNCY BANDIT KNOWN AS "LEAPIN' LENA," WE WILL DRAW SOME PICTURES -- INASMUCH AS WE'RE TEMPORARILY OUT OF DIAGRAMS.

THIS IS GOOSEQUILL McFARTHINGALE -- FAMED BROADJUMPER.

AND THIS--(UGH!)--IS SPRING UPANDOWNE...FAMED HIGH-JUMPER.

THE TWO RAN INTO ONE ANOTHER, YEARS AGO, AT A CONTEST STAGED BY THE ACROBATS' MARCHING AND CHOWDER CLUB...
YOW!
BANG!
-SIR?!

IT WAS A CASE OF LOVE AT FIRST FRIGHT.
YOU'RE BEAUTIFUL! - (PANT!) - MARRY ME...OR...I'LL NEVER BROAD-JUMP AGAIN!
HOORAY!! - HE'S OUT O' HIS MIND! - I'LL TAKE UP HIS OFFER B'FORE HE RETURNS TO HIS SENSES!

OUT OF THIS UNION OF CHAMPION BROAD-JUMPER AND CHAMPION HIGH-JUMPER EMERGED "LEAPIN' LENA" -- THE HUMAN KANGAROO --WHO HAS CHOSEN TO DIRECT HER REMARKABLE LEAPING TALENTS INTO CHANNELS OF CRIME!
2

CORNERED! -I'LL DUCK THESE SQUARES WITH A SURPRISE ANGLE!
ESCALATOR

AND ON THAT VERY SAME ESCALATOR ... ACE COMEDIAN LARRY DAVIS, ACCOMPANIED BY JUNE FARRELL, HIS BEAUTEOUS MANAGER.
YOU NEEDN'T LOOK SO BORED. IT ISN'T OFTEN I ASK YOU TO ACCOMPANY ME ON A SHOPPING EXPEDITION.
(YAWN!) - THIS IS PROBABLY THE DULLEST DAY OF MY LIFE.
CHEER UP, LARRY! 'TWON'T BE FOR LONG!

GOT TH' LOOT -- BUT I STILL GOTTA EVADE TH' LAW!
STOP THAT WOMAN!!
ESCALAT

YOU LOOK RITZY -- MIGHT BE RICH-TAKIN'S IN THAT POCKET BOOK!
LARRY! I'VE BEEN ROBBED!

GOOD GRIEF! OUR ONE-AND-ONLY COPY OF THE SCRIPT FOR TOMORROW'S BROADCAST IS IN THAT POCKETBOOK!
THEN WE'VE GOT TO GET IT BACK! - GANGWAY!

BUT AS LARRY AND THE STORE-DETECTIVES REACH THE SECOND FLOOR . . .
TH' TROUBLE WITH YOU'N IS YER ALL WRAPPED UP IN YERSELFS!
AGH!
TAKE IT OFF!

UNDER COVER OF THE SCREENING CLOTH, LARRY DAVIS REVERSES GARMENTS. - INTO VIEW SPRINGS . . . FUNNYMAN!
WHAT "LEAPIN' LENA" NEEDS IS A GOOD CRANK -- AN' THAT'S WHERE I COME IN!
3

FUNNYMAN!
REET!
GLOVES
STICK AROUND, FOLKS, FOR THE BATTLE OF THE NON-SENSURY!

NAUGHTY, NAUGHTY! - TH' LAW'S HOT ON YER TRAIL, SO IT'S TH' COOLER FER YA!
H'YAW! - YOU'VE BAD-NEWS T'NIGHT! NOBODY CAN SLAP THEIR MITTS ON "LEAPIN' LENA"!

AWRK! I'M SAPOTAGED!
I'M LIABLE T' SPRING ANYTHING!

BL-LUNK
WHOOOF-FF!!
H'YAW! H'YAW!
SHIRTS

OOF! ("-LAFF AT ME, WILL SHE? I'LL SHOW THAT HUMAN ANIMATED CARTOON A THING OR THREE!-")

HAW! HAW! -GOTCHA!
I'M A-HEADIN' FER TH' LAST CRACK-UP... TA-TA-DE-DUM ...DEE-DA...
4

THIS-A-WAY, LAW-LADS! I'VE CAPTURED TH' CATAPULTIN' CRITTER!
HMM-MMMM.....
FOR FIRE ONLY
TURN RIGHT

A TURN TO THE RIGHT...
OR ONLY
RIGHT

FOR FIRE ONLY

THE CHASE GOES ON!
GRR-RR!
(CACKLE!)
TREADMILL

AND ON!
THAT WONDERFUL STINK! WHAT IS IT???
IT'S PERFUME -- NAMED "I SURRENDER"-- GUARANTEED TO MAKE MAN OR BEAST WILT! - SURRENDER, BEAST!!!

TAKE A WHIFF O' "UNCONQUERED"!.. MY FAVORITE PERFUME!

YEP, YOU'RE RIGHT! AS OF NOW, THE FREE-FOR-ALL GAME OF TAG HAS FAILED TO TERMINATE. IN OTHER WORDS, MOE -- DON'T LAY DOWN THAT FUNNY BOOK...YET!
(PANT!-PANT!) -ODD! NO SIGHT O' FUNNYMAN! - DIDN'T THINK TH' SQUIRT WOULD GIVE UP SO EASY-LIKE!
("-HA!... STRATEGY!-")
RTRAIT UCHING

TEE HEE! NEVER COULD RESIST PAINTING MOUSTACHES 'ON PITCHERS!
HEY!
GOO'NESS ME! IT TALKS!
BLUB!!
TOODLE-OO BUB!
THINK YER RUNNIN' OUT, EH? SISTER, YER GONNA ESCAPE ME NEVER!
SORRY T' OF KEPT YA WAITIN', MONK AN' PUNK.
S'OKAY! BUT LE'S BEAT IT!
BUT HURTLING IN PURSUIT--THAT DARING DOPE...FUNNYMAN!
CROOKS! BANDITS! LOUTS! - HOLD YER GROUND! FUNNYMAN'S A-COMIN' FER TH' LAST ROUND-UP!!
6
ONE FALSE MOVE, AN' WE'LL BLOW YER BRAINS OUT!
YA SURE HAVE GOT AN ODD SENSE O' DIRECTION!

CRACK WISE, HUH? – TAKE DAT!
NO! DON'T SHOOT!
BANG
BANG
WHY'D YA DO IT, MONK? HE'S SO --(SIGH!) --PURTY!
AHH-HHHHH, STOW DEM TEARS AN' LE'S BEAT IT WID DA LOOT!
BUT AS THE CROOKED TRIO TURN TO DEPART.
DROP THOSE GUNS!!
ELEVATOR
B-BUT YOU'RE SUPPOSED T'BE DEAD!
IN TH' HEAD, YES --BUT THIS LI'L OL' METAL PLATE WENT AN' SAVED M' LIFE!
7
AND SO FUNNYMAN TURNED LENA AND HER MOBSTER ACCOMPLICES OVER TO THE POLICE. LATER--AS LARRY DAVIS...
HERE'S YOUR POCKETBOOK BACK --TOGETHER WITH THE MISSING SCRIPT. ...ANY COMMENTS?
OKAY. SO FUNNYMAN'S NOT SUCH A BAD EGG, AT THAT. BUT KINDLY DO NOT REMIND ME OF IT ANY MORE THAN NECESSARY!
THE END.

"The Peculiar Pacifier!" (*Funnyman* #5 July 1948)

AND SO A DISTRESSED TORGO SETS FORTH ON HIS UNHAPPIEST ERRAND.
I DON'T LIKE DIS NO-HOW! BUT --ORDERS IS ORDERS!
LETTER
U.S. MAIL

PS-ST! - YOO-HOO!!
TORGO...DOC GIMMICK'S BONEHEAD ASSISTANT!!!

STOP, OR YOU'RE A DEAD MAN!
(GR-ROAN!) TA T'INK I AST FER DIS!
BANG! BANG!

AH-HA! ...DOC GIMMICK! RAISE YOUR HANDS, YOU RATS!
TRAPPED!

WOTTA BREAK! EVERY OFFICER IN THE NATION IS ON THE LOOKOUT FOR YOU SCOUNDRELS, AND I CAPTURED YOU!
(GULP!)
OOPS! THE GLOBE SLIPPED!
2

(COUGH!) -I...I...
THE GLOBE BROKE!
WATCH CLOSELY --AND YOU'LL OBSERVE -- "THE PECULIAR PACIFIER"-- IN ACTION!

TCH! TCH! THERE I GO -- POINTING MY GUN AT PEOPLE, AGAIN! I'D BETTER PUT IT AWAY BEFORE SOMEONE GETS HURT.
AN EXCELLENT THOUGHT.
HUH?
PLEASE ACCEPT MY APOLOGY FOR TRYING TO JAIL YOU AND TORGO. IT WON'T HAPPEN AGAIN. AM I - ER- FORGIVEN??
HA! HA! -- WHY NOT?
WELL... GOT TO BE GOING NOW. S'LONG, FRIENDS!
BUT HE'S A COP, AN' WE'RE A COUPLE O' CROOKED SKUNKS! YET HE CALLS US FRIENDS! AN' A FEW MINUTES AGO HE WAS GONNA RUN US IN!
RELAX, TORGO. -I'LL EXPLAIN.
"THE PECULIAR PACIFIER" IS A NEW TYPE GAS I'VE INVENTED. ITS EFFECT ON PEOPLE IS TO MAKE THEM CONCILIATORY -- PEACEABLE! WHAT YOU'VE JUST WITNESSED WAS MERELY A TEST.
DO YOU REALIZE WHAT SUCH A DISCOVERY MEANS IN THE REALM OF CRIME? WE'LL BE ABLE TO ROB WHOEVER AND WHEREVER WE PLEASE... WITHOUT AN IOTA OF RESISTANCE!
YEAH -- I GET IT! HO! HO! IT'LL MAKE CRIME DA SAFEST PROFESSION ON EARTH!
3
MEANWHILE -- THE PENTHOUSE OF ACE COMEDIAN, LARRY DAVIS.
TCH! TCH! IS THIS HUMOR? I'M REFERRING TO THE "LOUIE THE LOUT" COMIC STRIP, OF COURSE.
OF COURSE!

GIMMIE DAT LOLLYPOP, "LOLLY," OR I'LL POP YA ONE!

BAWW-WW!

FOR SHEER GRUESOMENESS AND BRUTALITY, "LOUIE THE LOUT" IS UNSURPASSED!

IT'S AMAZING WHAT THE GREAT AMERICAN PUBLIC WILL STAND FOR IN THE NAME OF "HUMOR".

MEANWHILE -- THE OFFICES OF "FOUL FEATURES SYNDICATE, INC."

HERE'RE THE FACTS OF LIFE, STRAIGHT FROM THE SHOULDER. YOU, KARL BORISLOFF, HAVE CAPITALIZED IN YOUR COMIC STRIP UPON THE MEAN AND SEAMY ASPECTS OF LIFE -- MURDERS, TORTURES, KNIFINGS, DOUBLECROSSES... AND YOU'VE ALWAYS PICTURED THEM IN ALMOST CLINICAL DETAIL.

RIGHT! REVOLTING SIGHTS ALWAYS DRAW A MORBID CROWD--AND NO ONE COULD EVER BE MORE REVOLTING THAN MY (UGH!) "HERO," "LOUIE THE LOUT"!

BUT I'VE ALARMING NEWS FOR YOU. THE PUBLIC'S TASTE HAS APPARENTLY SWUNG BACK TO CLEAN, WHOLESOME STRIP-HEROES -- LIKE IN "BRINGING UP BROTHER" AND "BRUNETTIE". -- "LOUIE THE LOUT" IS HEADED FOR OBLIVION!

(PANT!) -WE CAN'T LET THAT HAPPEN! -I'D HAVE TO SELL MY STABLES... MY EIGHT MANSIONS ... AND GO BACK TO WASHING DISHES AT SAM'S SLOP-HOUSE...

MARK SADE COMICS ED.

I'VE WRACKED MY BRAIN... AND COME UP WITH THE ONLY SOLUTION. - YOU'VE GOT TO DREAM UP A NEW SEQUENCE WHICH IS MORE SICKENING, MORE GRUESOME, AND MORE REVOLTING THAN ALL PAST EPISODES! IF WE CAN SUCCEED IN GETTING "LOUIE THE LOUT" BANNED IN BOSTON, WE'LL GET TONS OF PUBLICITY... AND GET BACK ALL THE PAPERS WE'VE LOST!

I'LL DO IT!

4

AND SO, BOYS AND GIRLS, KARL BORISLOFF STRIKES THE LOWEST... WHICH TO HIM IS THE HIGHEST... DEPTHS OF HIS CAREER!

BOSTON.
I'VE RECEIVED A HOT TIP THAT A VALUABLE SHIPMENT OF GEMS IS TO BE STORED IN A BOSTON CITY BANK SAFETY-BOX THIS AFTERNOON.
WE'LL GRAB IT WID "DA PECULIAR PACIFIER", HAH?
LOUNGING WITHIN EARSHOT--LARRY DAVIS--WHO HAS DROPPED INTO TOWN FOR A ONE-NIGHT APPEARANCE.
DOC GIMMICK AND TORGO--UP TO DIRTY DOINGS!!
LARRY! IF YOU'RE THINKING OF ADOPTING THAT FUNNYMAN ROUTINE AGAIN... I... I'LL...!
LATER THAT AFTERNOON.
BANK
PS-ST! HERE COMES THE MESSENGER WITH THE GEMS! QUICK! SLIP IT TO ME, TORGO!
HAW! HAW! - ONE "PECULIAR PACIFIER," COMIN' UP!!
HOLD IT! - KNOW TH' TIME, BUB?
IT'S 2 O'CLOCK. - YIKE - FUNNYMAN!!!
"THE PECULIAR PACIFIER"! - I'LL USE IT TO RENDER THE GOOFY GUMSHOE HARMLESS!
HO! HO! HO! - YA MISSED!
5
AS FATE WOULD HAVE IT -- "THE PECULIAR PACIFIER" HURTLES STRAIGHT TOWARD THE OPEN WINDOW OF THE EDITORIAL ROOM OF "THE BOSTON DAILY PRESS"...
...JUST AS MANAGING EDITOR B. BEANE IS ABOUT TO SURVEY THE LATEST BATCH OF "LOUIE THE LOUT" ADVANCE PROOFS.
IT WAS AN ERROR TO RUN THE MONSTROSITY IN THE FIRST PLACE. UNLESS THERE'S BEEN CONSIDERABLE IMPROVEMENT IN THE FEATURE'S MORAL TONE, OUT IT GOES!

AND NOW, WITH YOUR PERMISSION, WE'LL TAKE A PEEK INTO A REPRESENTATIVE GROUP OF NEWSPAPER OFFICES THROUGHOUT THE NATION. FIRST, THE CLEVELAND CLARION.
CANCEL "LOUIE THE LOUT"! THAT MADMAN BORISLOFF HAS FINALLY GONE TOO FAR!
RIP
EDITOR

THE ST. LOUIS SENTINEL.
NO ONE --(GASP!)-- MUST EVER SEE THESE FIENDISH CONCOCTIONS! - CANCEL "LOUIE THE LOUT"!

AND AS CLEVELAND AND ST. LOUIS GOES, SO GOES THE NATION!
KILL THAT STRIP!
UNFIT FOR PRINT!
GIVE IT TH HOOK!!

BUT IN THE OFFICES OF "THE BOSTON DAILY PRESS"--AS "THE PECULIAR PACIFIER" DOES ITS STUFF...
DELIGHTFUL! - QUAINT! - HEH, HEH! THE SCOUNDREL STEALS HIS MOTHER'S LIFE SAVINGS! - PRICELESS! - WE'LL RUN IT ON THE FRONT PAGE!

MEANWHILE.
HA! WON'T MISS YOU THIS TIME!
N'YA! N'YA!! - I CAUGHT IT!
6

RIGHT BACK!
GET HIM, TORGO! GET HIM!!!
ARGH!

PUT 'EM UP, YA NAUGHTY NO-GOODS! I'M READY -- FISTS, TOOTSIES, 'N' ALL!!
US? FIGHT YOU??
DEAR ME, NO!

WE WOULDN'T DREAM OF IT!
NOT IN A MILYUN YEARS!
??

OFFICER! COME HERE! PLEASE ARREST TORGO AND ME! WE WERE ABOUT TO COMMIT A ROBBERY!
AN' THAS A VERRR-RRRY BAD THING!
NOW I'VE SEEN EVERYTHING!

I STILL DON'T GET IT! - BUT- HYAWWW-HAWWW-HAW! - WHAT DOES IT MATTER AS LONG AS THOSE BUMS GET RUSHED TO A CELL??
7

BUT WHAT OF "LOUIE THE LOUT"? AND "FOUL FEATURES SYNDICATE, INC."? AND KARL BORISLOFF?
EVERY ONE OF OUR NEWSPAPER CLIENTS CANCELLED EXCEPT BOSTON!
WHICH SEALS OUR DOOM! -I'VE BEEN APPROVED IN BOSTON! -GAD! I'LL NEVER LIVE IT DOWN!!
MARKSADE COMICS ED.
THE END.

FUNNYMAN #1

(January 1948)

Origin Page: [See Page 9.]

1. ***The Teen-Age Terrors!*** Hollywood starlet Darlene Dalrymple and Hankie Sonota (a Frank Sinatra stand-in) are robbed by teen fans. A few days later, Larry Davis is breaking them up at the The Comedian's Club. On the street, autograph-seeking kids palm his family heirloom watch. Larry chases them to a waterfront warehouse. There he spies the exchange of his watch to Ants Pants and his lowlife gang. They plan to sell it to Fencie Finnegan. Davis dons his rubber nose and clown pants as Funnyman. He tumbles into their lair and hides under a table after retrieving his watch. The teens think one of them has snatched it and they rumble, knocking over the table, which reveals the Comic Crimebuster. He is tied up and about to be tossed in the river. Funnyman kicks the hooligan into the water instead and is dragged back into their HQ. The bound Funnyman manages to turn the knob on the gas heater. Tied to a chair, he confuses the mob as they pass out from the fumes. June leads the cops to Anty's hideout. Taking June's car, the Daffy Daredevil races to Fencie's shack. On the way, he dukes it out with Antsy. Back at his apartment, June, "the Brain," presents Larry with his precious heirloom. The J.D.s took a cheap imitation watch, which June placed on Larry's wrist.

FUNNYMAN
by JERRY SIEGEL AND JOE SHUSTER
IS EVERYBODY SLAPHAPPY? IF YOU'RE READY FOR LAUGHS AND THRILLS, DON YOUR BROADEST GRIN AND PREPARE TO RACE ALONG THE DANGER TRAIL WITH FUNNYMAN AS THE PLANET'S FUNNIEST SLEUTH MATCHES MISCHIEVOUS MIRTH AGAINST THE MALICIOUS MAYHEM OF...
"THE TEEN-AGE TERRORS!"
HA! HA! HOW DOES IT FEEL TO BE HEADED FOR A CRUSHING DEFEAT?
CLOUT ME, IF YOU MUST! BUT LAY OFF THE GAGS. THAT'S MY RACKET!
3822
1

2. ***Funnyman, Comicman, and Laffman.*** Two costumed imitators of Funnyman, the rotund Laffman and the elfish Comicman seek to capture the fugitive Flathead Floogie. After dispatching his irritating, smug competitors, Funnyman brings Floogie to justice.

3. ***Funnyman, Comicman, and Laffman.*** Flathead Floogie escapes from the police at Grand Central Station. While Larry Davis puts on his Funnyman attire, two other comic crusaders, Laffman and Comicman, transform into their crime-busting personae. The trio capture Flathead by the railroad tracks but Funnyman brushes off his cheap imitators and returns the arch-criminal to the authorities.

4. ***The Truant Toy.*** Larry buys a toy kangaroo on his way to a nightclub performance. A sneak thief goes backstage and manhandles June. The Dippy Hipster throws ink and assorted junk at the mean-spirited crook. For safekeeping, June has secreted her diamond ring in the mechanical toy, which tears across the cityscape, now chased by Funnyman. Finally in the Empire City Zoo, the Daffy Detective apprehends the errant windup kangaroo and returns the ring to June. After the show, an exuberant Larry purchases five mechanical dogs.

FUNNYMAN #2

(March 1948)

1. ***The Crime-Car.*** The inventor Sardonic Lazar strikes again with his notorious Crime-Car, bowling over police vehicles and smashing into stores for their loot. Meanwhile at Larry Davis' estate, the master showman reveals his Jet-Jalopy to June and Happy. Astonishingly, the junkmobile responds to Larry's every command and can tumble over land, sea, and sky. Seeding along in his Crime-Car, Lazar challenges the Slaphappy Slugger to an auto battle royale. The Daffy Daredevil makes mincemeat of Lazar's gang as his Metal Monster rescues him from being pulverized and signals the police to Lazar's whereabouts.

2. ***A Fool's Duel!*** In Ventral Park, Larry overhears a young woman, Dolores, pleading with her lover to flee. France's Greatest Duelist, Charles Cheval has threatened to dispatch any rival for Dolores' hand. Funnyman decides to teach the foreign "no-goodnick" a lesson in proper American etiquette. He drops an egg on the Frenchman's head and besoils his elegant suit. The suave Monsieur challenges the Ace Comedian to a fencing match. Funnyman's sword, however, is useless, a wooden replica. Cheval stabs the Daffy Daredevil

IMITATION MAY BE THE SINCEREST FORM OF FLATTERY, BUT IT'S ALSO A FINE JUSTIFICATION FOR MAYHEM! WHEN UNINSPIRED IMITATORS CUT IN ON THE **COMIC CRIMEBUSTER'S** CUT-UPS, OUR FRIVOLOUS FRIEND, NATCH, BLOWS HIS TOP! ALL THIS AND FISTI-CUFFS, TOO, IN THE BATTLE GALORE BETWIXT........................

FUNNYMAN, COMICMAN and LAFFMAN

in the heart—really a bag of red ink. Infuriated, Dolores' companion slugs the Frenchman to the ground as Funnyman slices his belt in half. The humiliated duelist shuffles away and Larry returns to the happy isolation of his park bench.

3. ***Slippery Slim!*** June and Larry pay a visit to Empire City's jail. Just as Sgt. Harrigan is about to lecture them on the latest "crook-nabbing" methods, it is announced that Slippery Slim, the "World's Slyest Jailbreaker," has escaped again. Slim corners Funnyman, knocks him out, exchanges clothing, and walks out of the police station in a perfect disguise. All is right until June kisses Slim and his putty nose drops off, revealing his true identity. Slippery Slim continues his flight but Funnyman smacks him off his guard. Naturally, the police gang up on the Muddlehead Trickster, thinking they have captured their felonious prey. In the end, June straightens them out and Larry, smirkingly, listens to Harrigan's boasts about his crime-detection brio.

4. ***Kute Knockout!*** [See Page 86.]

FUNNYMAN #3

(April 1948)

1. ***The Timid Menace.*** An impish, red-suited alien, Tamidio from the Planet Dearth, lands in the center of Empire City. As a crowd gathers, the bald creator explains his interplanetary mission: to gain control of Earth. A smarmy reporter, Orville Smelles, drives the little guy to the newsroom of the *Daily Graphic*. He convinces his editor that the delusional hoaxer will be an immediate headline sensation. Sure enough, Tamidio becomes an overnight amusement. He even unintentionally bests Larry as a laugh-getter at an outdoor charity event. Tossed off a dock, Tamidio exacts vengance with a lightning storm. Funnyman chases him across the riverbank and Tamidio transports him to the Planet Dearth. At their Council Hall, Funnyman manically performs an array of practical jokes, which frighten Dearth's leaders. One of the Council members interrogates Funnyman about his life's goals. The Screwball Scrapper delivers his Earthling Manifesto: to make enough money, after taxes, to purchase a few minor luxuries and a corner beer. The Dearthers are so startled by his smart-alec philosophy that they decide not to invade Earth and send its jester back home.

anc
FUNNYMAN
by
JERRY SIEGEL
JOE SHUSTER
10c
No. 3
APRIL 1948
KARAT
JEWELER
CO.

2. ***The House That Funnyman Built.*** A new mob, led by Giggles Cain, plan to kill Funnyman in order to ensure the success of their racket scheme. They wound the Silly Sleuth but he manages to drive his Trix-Cycle back to Funnymanor. Cain's gang follows him to the weird abode. Like a funhouse environment, every room in Funnymanor frustrates their murderous abilities. Finally, Giggles and his team are bound and frog-marched to a police precinct.

3. ***When Gadgeteers Clash.*** Doc Gimmick and a crooked baseball player, Hew-Haw Johnson bust out of prison, using one of Doc's sky-piercing inventions. At a charity carnival, Funnyman appears as a ball-toss target. Johnson tries to bean the Laughing Lad with an explosive hardball. In the ensuing battle, Funnyman is trapped in a lion's cage and dumped into the sea. At the Fighting Fool's funeral, Funnyman leaps out of his coffin to capture Doc Gimmick, his gloating nemesis. Our hero then explains his narrow escape—he secured the wire cage to a tree just before the flat dropped off the cliff.

4. ***For the Honor of Sgt. Harrigan.*** In order to disrupt Sgt. Harrigan's Testimonial Dinner for 20 years of service, Slippery Slim digs his way out of prison. At the dinner hall, Funnyman mouths his usual wisenheimer insults. While a guest speaker tangles with the red-nosed interloper, Slim pockets Harrigan's silver loving cup. The Grinnin' Goof leaps after him, recovering the cup and vanquishing Slim. Harrigan complains that Funnyman has once again stolen his glory.

FUNNYMAN #4

(May 1948)

1. ***Medieval Mirthquake.*** [See Page 91.]

2. ***The Return of Slippery Slim.*** An expert jail-breaker, Slippery Slim once again manages to outwit Sgt. Harrigan and spring himself from the city slammer. Slim dashes out of Police Headquarters, wearing Harrigan's uniform, but Larry Davis recognizes Slim's camouflage and changes into Funnyman mode. After cornering the felon in an alley, Harrigan crashes into Funnyman and Slim escapes. Inspector Bliss berates Harrigan and gives him 48 hours to recapture the slippery con. Meanwhile, Davis prepares to avenge Harrigan's loss. The next day in an underworld dive, the egotistic Slim reads that Boris Porous, the addled film producer of "Gone With the Breeze," has announced that Harrigan will portray the arch-criminal in his next super-epic based on Slim's jail-breaking career. But Harrigan refuses Porous' offer, although Pierre Blintz, the costumer, and Lucille Schlemiel, the makeup artist, are attached to the deal. Suddenly Slim breaks into Harrigan's office and demands to play himself. Porous' beret and goatee fall to the floor. It is Funnyman in an artful disguise. He knocks out Slim and razes Harrigan before jumping out the window.

3. ***Leapin' Lena.*** [See Page 106.]

FUNNYMAN #5

(July 1948)

1. ***Wanted: One Corpse!*** After stealing millions of dollars, Louie the Louse bemoans his current fate to his gang—Lola, Peanut, and Thimblebrain: the police, knowing about the theft, will be shadowing his every move. Louis brainstorms a solution; if his underlings

No. 5
FUNNYMAN
by JERRY SIEGEL and JOE SHUSTER
JULY 1948
10c

No. 6
FUNNYMAN
by
JERRY SIEGEL and JOE SHUSTER
AUGUST 1948
10c
CANDY

can find a man with similar bodily features to the Louse, he can have Dr. Hacksaw alter the stoolie's face and fingerprints to surgically replicate his appearance and then murder him. As soon as the cops discover Louis' dead look-alike, their search will cease. Lola, the blonde fatale, hunts down a first sucker but his head is larger than Louis'. Then Funnyman tumbles into her clutches. Lola drags the besmitten fall guy to Louis' hideaway. She blindfolds him for a game of spin-the-bottle. But Sgt. Harrigan interrupts her ruse and the Comic Crimebuster escapes only to be nabbed by the gang again. They escort him to Louis' office, where the Fighting Fool subdues the gang with his laughing gas pistol.

2. ***Downfall of Noodnik Nogoodnik.*** While June Farrel and Happy prepare a novel twist to Larry Davis' next comedy routine, the Daffy Daredevil spies Noodnik Nogodnik stealing money from Little Jimmy Zito, an orphaned shoeshine boy. Funnyman leaps from his apartment and rescues Jimmy and his dog, Ragsy, from further abuse. He tangles with Noodnik and discovers that Jimmy was kidnapped from a wealthy family many years ago. The red-nosed crusader delivers Noodnik to the Empire City jail and the long-lost Jimmy to his now grateful mother.

3. ***Peculiar Pacifier.*** [See Page 113.]

FUNNYMAN #6

(August 1948)

1. ***The Super Snooper.*** In the municipal library, Larry discovers a newspaper item from 1938. Schemer Beamer was convicted of stealing the Mafoosky Gems and sentenced to ten years in a federal penitentiary. The Screwball Scrapper realizes that the unrepentant thief will soon rejoin his mobster associates—Rockjaw, Crusher, and The Curve. But in the waning decade, the gang has changed; the boys have considerably weakened and The Curve has put on a few pounds. They jump into a beat-up convertible, only to discover Funnyman is their chauffeur. He takes them for a wild drive into an elevator entrance of an old building. After many unsuccessful attempts to dispose of the Laughing Loon, they are apprehended with a crate of the Mafoosky jewels. A jealous Sgt. Harrigan kicks Funnyman's steel-plated behind.

2. ***The Birthday Party.*** Slippery Slim escapes from a police tvan and runs into Funnyman on his motorcycle. After duking it out, Slim slips into the window of a nearby house.

Funnyman follows in hot pursuit and interrupts a sputtering children's birthday party. The kids implore the Dashing Daredevil to join their festivities, which he does. One of the girls leads the Big Infant into a dark room for a game of Post Office. Instead of a kiss, Funnyman gets walloped on the head by Slim. Later our Dynamic Dope wrestles down Slim during a Pin-the-Tail-On-the-Donkey free-for-all.

FUNNYMAN
SUNDAY STRIPS

"The Many Faces of Piccadilly Pete" (October 31, 1948)

HE'LL ESCAPE! UNLESS...!
BL-LAM

DOWN UPON PICCADILLY PETE CASCADES A SHOWER OF PHONY MONEY.
MONEY! MONEY!! MONEY!!!

THE CROOK'S GREED LEADS TO HIS DOWNFALL!
MINE! ALL MINE!!

KONK!
COMIC CROOK C

EN ROUTE TO POLICE HEAD-QUARTERS!
BAH!
I'M TH' WORLD'S TOUGHEST HERO -- BUT MY I.Q. IS ZERO! THA'S WHY I'M CALLED FUNNYMAN!!
YAK! YAK!
To the CLINK
COMIC CROOK-CATCHER
11-14-48

"The Tunesmith Caper" (December 5, 1948-January 2, 1949) p. 121

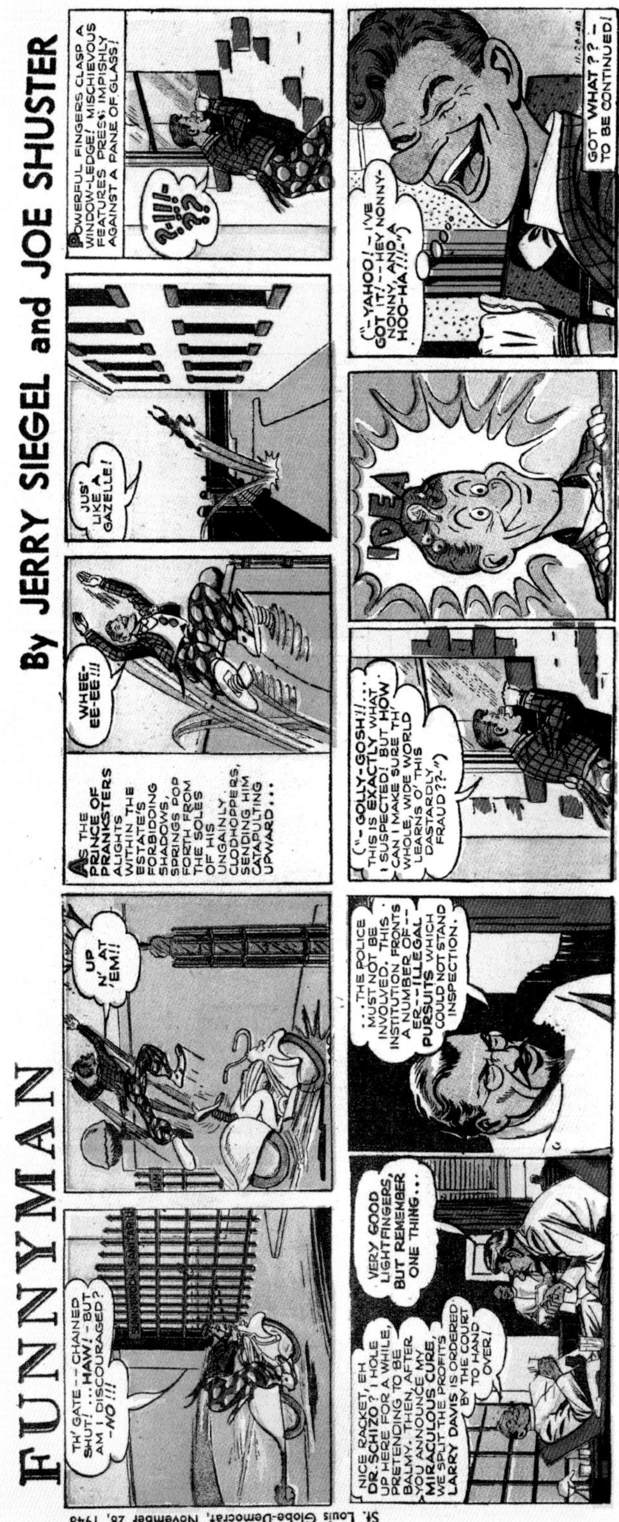

St. Louis Globe-Democrat, November 28, 1948

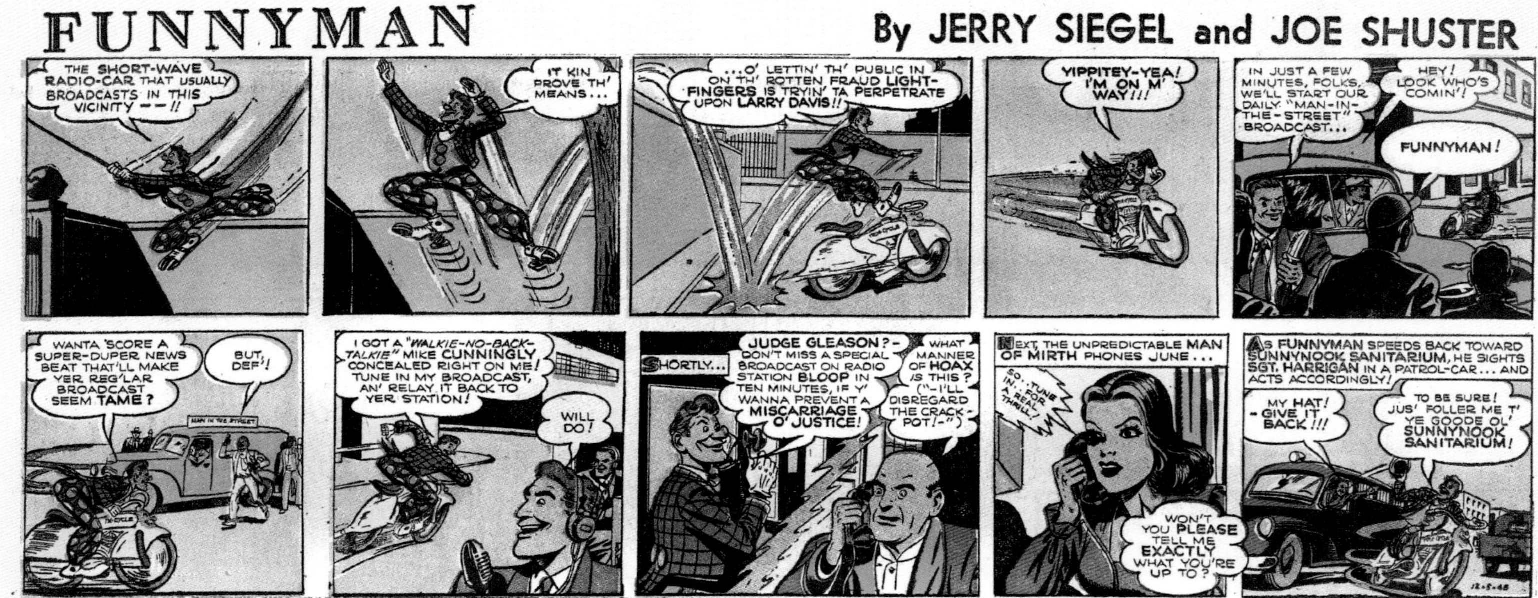
FUNNYMAN
By JERRY SIEGEL and JOE SHUSTER
THE SHORT-WAVE RADIO-CAR THAT USUALLY BROADCASTS IN THIS VICINITY --!!
IT KIN PROVE TH' MEANS...
...O' LETTIN' TH' PUBLIC IN ON TH' ROTTEN FRAUD LIGHT-FINGERS IS TRYIN' TA PERPETRATE UPON LARRY DAVIS!!
YIPPITEY-YEA! I'M ON M' WAY!!!
IN JUST A FEW MINUTES, FOLKS, WE'LL START OUR DAILY "MAN-IN-THE-STREET" BROADCAST...
HEY! LOOK WHO'S COMIN'!
FUNNYMAN!
WANTA 'SCORE A SUPER-DUPER NEWS BEAT THAT'LL MAKE YER REG'LAR BROADCAST SEEM TAME?
BUT, DEF'!
I GOT A "WALKIE-NO-BACK-TALKIE" MIKE CUNNINGLY CONCEALED RIGHT ON ME! TUNE IN MY BROADCAST, AN' RELAY IT BACK TO YER STATION!
WILL DO!
SHORTLY...
JUDGE GLEASON?- DON'T MISS A SPECIAL BROADCAST ON RADIO STATION BLOOP IN TEN MINUTES, IF Y' WANNA PREVENT A MISCARRIAGE O' JUSTICE!
WHAT MANNER OF HOAX IS THIS? ("-I'LL DISREGARD THE CRACK-POT!-")
NEXT, THE UNPREDICTABLE MAN OF MIRTH PHONES JUNE...
SO...TUNE IN...FOR A REAL THRILL!
WON'T YOU PLEASE TELL ME EXACTLY WHAT YOU'RE UP TO?
AS FUNNYMAN SPEEDS BACK TOWARD SUNNYNOOK SANITARIUM, HE SIGHTS SGT. HARRIGAN IN A PATROL-CAR... AND ACTS ACCORDINGLY!
MY HAT! -GIVE IT BACK!!!
TO BE SURE! JUS' FOLLER ME T' YE GOODE OL' SUNNYNOOK SANITARIUM!
12-5-48

FUNNYMAN

By JERRY SIEGEL and JOE SHUSTER

STOP-- YOU--YOU HAT-THIEF!
-HYAW! HYAW! -TEMPER, TEMPER, SARGIE-WARGIE!

GR-R-RR! THAT GOOFY GUMSHOE HAS GONE TOO FAR, THIS TIME! I'LL ARREST 'IM FOR BEIN' A PUBLIC NUISANCE!
BUT FIRST Y'LL HAFTA CATCH HIM!

SUCTION-CUP EQUIPPED TIRES CARRY THE SLAPSTICK SLEUTH RIGHT UP THE SIDE OF THE WALL SURROUNDING THE SUNNYNOOK ESTATE.
UP-'N-OVER!!

HERE'S ONE WOOSMAN WHO WON'T SPARE THE TREE!!

TIM-BERRR!!!

CRASH!

EH? - WHAT WAS THAT?
AN EARTHQUAKE?!!

READY OR NOT, HERE I COME!

YA-HOO!

12-12-48

HYAK! HYAK! -GOOD EVENIN', FRIENDS!!
POW!

FUNNYMAN
By JERRY SIEGEL and JOE SHUSTER
AS FUNNYMAN SWITCHES ON THE "WALKIE-NO-BACK-TALKIE" CONCEALED IN HIS TROUSERS...!
WOW! FUNNYMAN WASN'T FOOLIN' ABOUT A SCOOP! HE'S BROAD-CASTING A BATTLE-ROYAL...!
AN' IT'S COMIN' THRU GREAT!
OPEN THAT GATE, LAD! I AIM TO LEARN WHAT'S GOIN' ON HERE! ("-AN' GET MY HAT BACK!-")
Y-YES, SIR! ("-BLAST IT! NO TIME T' WARN DR. SHIZO!-")
OVERPOWER HIM!
HERE'S WHERE I BOWL YOU OVER WITH SOME BOLOS!
HAAA-HA-HAA-AA!
("-I'LL STIFLE THAT MADDENING LAUGHTER!-")
UNEXPECTEDLY REACHING IN, THE SLAPSTICK SLUGGER GRABS DR. SHIZO'S ELBOWS--AND YANKS DOWN!
TCH! TCH! SUCH LAN-GWIDGE!!
WANT IT OFF? HAPPY T' OBLIGE!
GR-ROAN!
CRASH
GR-ROAN!
HYAW! HAW-WW!!
THE AUDACIOUS FIGHTING FOOL! THERE MUST BE A METHOD TO HIS MAD-NESS, BUT WILL HE COME OUT OF THE BATTLE ALIVE?!
HO! HO!! - ARE YOU FLOORED! ("-I FEEL GREAT! WHEN JUDGE GLEASON HEARS WHAT'S COMIN' UP, LARRY DAVIS'LL BE CLEARED!-")
BUT WHAT POOR FUNNYMAN CAN-NOT KNOW IS THAT AT THIS VERY INSTANT THE EMINENT MAGISTRATE IS DOZING OFF INTO DREAMLAND...!
SO...Z-ZZZ... SLEEPY...

FUNNYMAN
By JERRY SIEGEL and JOE SHUSTER
HAA-HAA-AA-A! -YOU'RE NEXT, YOU LUCKY LAD, YOU!!
WH-WHAT DO YOU WANT OF ME?
NOT MUCH, CHUM! JUS'A CONFESSION ADMITTIN' YOU'VE BIN FEIGNIN' MADNESS SO AS T' SNATCH "PIDDLE-DADDLE GLOOK" PROFITS FROM JERKIMER JONES AN' LARRY DAVIS!
MEANWHILE....
CAN'T SLEEP--KEEP WONDERING WHETHER OR NOT THAT WAS A CRANK WHO CALLED, AFTER ALL. ONLY ONE WAY TO FIND OUT...
IT'S--IT'S TRUE! I'VE PRETENDED I'M BALMY SO THAT THE OLD PRACTICAL-JOKE CONTRACT WITH JERKIMER JONES WOULD STAND UP IN COURT! -K-KEEP AWAY!!
...IN COURT! -K-KEEP AWAY!!
??? - THAT DOESN'T SOUND LIKE A REHEARSED RADIO DRAMA! - PERHAPS...?!!
GOT HIM!!
YAA-A A-A
FUNNYMAN'S HIDDEN "WALKIE-TALKIE" STOPS THE BULLET--BUT IS DESTROYED.
OO-FF!
YOU HAVE JUST HEARD A SHORT-WAVE BROADCAST OF FUNNYMAN ACTUALLY CLASHING WITH DANGEROUS CRIMINALS! IT WAS UNEXPECTEDLY BROKEN OFF. HE MAY BE IN DIRE PERIL!
OH!
HE KNOWS TOO MUCH! WE MUST RID OURSELVES OF HIM PERMANENTLY!
TAKE HIM TO THE BASEMENT FURNACE!
DON'T MOVE!
DA COPS!!
CRASH!

FUNNYMAN
By JERRY SIEGEL and JOE SHUSTER
STICK 'EM UP, COPPER—YOU'RE COVERED!!
LET'S CLEAR OUT, SHIZO! THE HEAT'S ON!!
SUDDENLY A STEEL WIRE SHOOTS OUT FROM FUNNYMAN'S WONDER-WEAPON -- THE FUNNYGUN!
ZING!
WHA— ?!!!
TRAPPED!
HA! HA! - DON'T BE ALARMED!! - IT'S JUS' ME SENDIN' YOU A WIRE!
POP!
HERE'S YER PRECIOUS HAT BACK, SARGE -- WITH A COUPLA MEAN CHARACTERS TOSSED IN FOR GOOD MEASURE!
BLAST IT! I DON'T KNOW WHETHER TO THANK YOU OR CUSS YOU!!
I'M TH' WORLD'S TOUGHEST HERO BUT MY I.Q. IS ZERO -- THAS WHY I'M CALLED FUNNYMAN!
YAK! YAK!
THAT SCREWBALL CRIMEBUSTER REALLY ISN'T SO BAD, IS HE, SERGEANT?
MEBBE SO! ("-WHO KNOWS? THESE ARRESTS MIGHT BRING ME A PROMOTION!-").
??-ROTTEN EGGS!!-- WHY... THAT SILLY SAPOTEUR! !... I...I COULD...!!!!
SEVERAL DAYS LATER.
NO DENYING IT, LARRY! FUNNYMAN DID A BEAUTIFUL JOB OF EXPOSING THAT LEGAL FRAUD!
LIGHTFINGERS AND HIS CRONIES FULLY DESERVED THE STIFF SENTENCES JUDGE GLEASON HANDED THEM!
I'VE A CONFESSION, KIDS. I'M SORRY I EVER FOISTED "PIDDLE-DADDLE GLOOK" ON THE UNSUSPECTING PUBLIC. THE MORONIC TUNE HAUNTS ME EVERY-WHERE I TURN!!
JERKIMER JONES TO SEE YOU, SIR. HE SAYS HE'S WRITTEN A NEW SONG HIT!
OH, NO!!
"GLEEP, GLEEP... I'M A CREEP!"
NO! NO!! - ANYTHING BUT THAT!!!

"June's Makeover" (March 20, 1949)

"The Mauler" (April 17, 1949)

The following is a partial list of Funnyman's Sunday page adventures.

October 31, 1948 to November 14, 1948. "The Many Faces of Piccadilly Pete."
Piccadilly Pete, "Briton's most notorious thief," uses various disguises to commit robberies. First he dresses in drag, robbing a bank, then as Inspector Healthcliff, the policeman who is trying to hunt him down. Funnyman penetrates his disguise and chases the thief down in his "Comic Crook-Catcher," a goofy machine with a crook-catching arm and front end that shoots a barrage of nails to give the thief's car flat tires.

December 5, 1948 to January 2, 1949. "The Tunesmith Caper."
Winston Lightfingers of Gypsum Music, Inc. copyrights a song written by Jerkimer Jones but refuses to pay an advance for it because the small print states that he must publish it "only if he is out of his mind." Larry Davis subsequently publishes it and the song becomes a hit. Lightfingers sues Larry for publishing it illegally, and the contract is upheld in court because Lightfingers was recently committed to a mental institution. Thus, Larry must pay all royalties to the shyster. The publisher feigns going insane and hides out in a mental hospital run by his crony, Dr. Schizo, and plans to announce a miracle cure and claim the profits ordered by the court. Funnyman decides to expose the crooks: to gain entrance, he drives up the side of the sanitarium with suction-cup tires and crashes through a window. After battling the crooks, Funnyman forces Lightfingers to admit his crime in a radio broadcast heard by the judge that tried the case. He wraps the crooks together with tape shot from his Funnygun and the police cart them off. Larry declares that he's sorry he ever published the moronic song and refuses to hear Jerkimer's new ditty but is serenaded by him through a window.

January 9, 1949 to January 30, 1949. "The Charity Bazaar Scam."
Doc Gimmick and his henchman Torgo are penniless bums in skid row. The criminal mastermind gets the idea to make a fortune through a bunko charity benefit for the "Society for Underprivileged Children." Larry Davis is a performer in the event and foils Doc's scheme just before he tries to remove Funnyman's fake nose and discover his true identity.

February 6. 1949 to March 13, 1949. "The Man With the Lisp."
A knife-throwing act turns murderous when the human target runs from the stage in fear and is knifed in the back. Before he dies he tells Larry that he is a secret serviceman on the trail of agents who threaten the United States with annihilation. Funnyman uncovers a plot by international spies, headed by a man with a lisp, to steal a new tiny, super-powerful atom bomb which could destroy America. They throw June from a high-rise girder but Funnyman rescues her, propelled by an elastic cord. Funnyman makes them surrender by threatening them with the bomb, but it turns out to be only an ant-bomb that June was going to use in her garden.

March 20, 1949. "June's Makeover."
To divert Larry's attention from the lovely ladies in town June buys a new dress, has a massage, an exercise workout, and gets a new hair-do. But the only thing Larry notices is that she's rearranged the furniture.

March 27, 1949 to April 17, 1949. "The Mauler."
The Mauler is a huge thug and leader of a gang of robbers. Funnyman defeats him through various humorous tricks and an uncharacteristic show of fisticuffs.

April 24, 1949. "June's Last Stand."
June tries to convince Larry to give up his career as a crime fighter but doesn't notice that he has disappeared to catch the robber who has stolen her purse and continues with her speech. Larry returns and agrees to her demand, not knowing what it is, and June mistakenly thinks she has won. She tells Larry, "Thanks—then it's settled. No More Funnyman!!" and congratulates herself for "outtalking" Larry for once.

May 1, 1949 to June 4, 1949. "McGlook's Challenge."
Luke McGlook places an article in the newspaper threatening Funnyman and daring Funnyman to meet him at the toy carnival. McGlook plans to ruin his career as a crime fighter by making a fool of him in public. McGlook hires a stage magician who challenges Funnyman to escape from a straitjacket from which no one has ever freed himself. McGlook then beats him up and threatens to rob the audience until the bound clown fights back.

July 3, 1949. "The Waif."

Larry Davis introduces a poor urchin named Peanuts Dolan to an adman who turns him into an advertising sensation because of his winning smile. Larry gets him a lucrative advertising contract with appearances on radio and in newsreels, and his picture on a multitude of products that bear his name.

August 7, 1949 to August 21, 1949. "Man's Best Friend."

Reggie Van Twerp begs Aunt Lucy to introduce him to Sally Howe whom he has fallen madly in love with. But he is thwarted in his amorous designs by Sally's Great Dane.

September 4, 1949 to September 25, 1949. "Princess Fatima."

At Farnum & Daily's Circus, Sam, a sideshow con man, tries to fleece Reggie by giving him a magic lantern that supposedly contains the gorgeous Princess Fatima, genie of the lamp, who will grant any wish he desires. When Reggie rubs the lamp and pronounces the magic word under the full moon, the "slave of the lamp" appears. Sam has his friend Maizie pose in a harem outfit as the princess. She asks Reggie for $10,000 to prove he is worthy of having his wishes granted. Reggie is such a dope that he'd rather have a piece of apple pie "like mom made" than a kiss from the princess, and Sam has to sock him and steal the loot. But Higgins has discovered the scheme and substituted a bag of bees for the cash.

October 9, 1949. "Spare the Rod."

Aunt Lucy brings her bratty young charge Milton over to Reggie's. When Milton bites Reggie's hand, Lucy won't let Reggie punish him because Milton goes to a "progressive" school where he is permitted to do exactly as he pleases so that he will "grow up free of repressions and feelings of inferiority." Milton proceeds to wreak havoc. When he tears up a stamp album, Lucy chides Reggie for objecting until she learns it is hers. She smacks Milton, proclaiming that she's going to quit the progressive school and send him to public school before he becomes a "completely impossible brat."

FUNNYMAN
DAILY STRIPS

"Adventures in Hollywood" (Daily Strip: January 13-March 19, 1949)

FUNNYMAN—By Jerry Siegel and Joe Shuster
A Bouncing Beau
LARRY'S CERTAINLY INSPIRED TONIGHT, ISN'T HE, HAPPY
HE'S AT HIS BEST, JUNE. AND THE AUDIENCE LOVES IT!
WHY LISTEN TO THAT CRUDE LOUT, LOLA... WHEN WE COULD GO TO SOME INSPIRING, ROMANTIC SETTING?
STOP BREATHING ON MY NECK.
BUT, LOLA, DEAREST! LIGHT OF MY...
OH, PLEASE STOP YAMMERING. YOU ANNOY ME. -- BROGAN, REMOVE THIS MAN!
THIS MEANS AN INTERNATIONAL INCIDENT!
OUT!
1-15-49
FUNNYMAN—By Jerry Siegel and Joe Shuster
A Woman Scorned
AT THE CLOSE OF THE STAGE SHOW.
LARRY DAVIS INTERESTS ME. BRING HIM HERE.
SORRY, MR. DAVIS ISN'T SEEING ANYONE RIGHT NOW.
LARRY DAVIS
LADY, MISS LEEDS IS TH' RICHEST WOMAN IN TH' WORLD. WHEN SHE WANTS TO SEE SOMEONE, THEY COME RUNNING!
AM I TO UNDERSTAND THAT THE VERY FAMOUS AND FABULOUS WEALTHY LOLA LEEDS WANTS TO SEE ME?
RIGHT, MISTER. SHALL WE GET GOIN'?
HE TOLD ME TO GIVE THIS TO YOU. SAID HE WAS TOO BUSY TO BRING IT HIMSELF.
HIS AUTO-GRAPH!!! ...SO HE'S PLAYING HARD TO GET, EH? (I'LL FIX HIM!)

FUNNYMAN—By Jerry Siegel and Joe Shuster
Attacked
MOST MEN WOULD HAVE SNAPPED AT THE OPPORTUNITY TO CHAT WITH AN ENORMOUSLY WEALTHY GIRL LIKE LOLA LEEDS!
I'M NOT IN A SNAPPING MOOD. ...'XCUSE ME, WHILE I STEP OUT INTO THE ALLEY FOR A BREATH OF FRESH AIR.
EXIT
EXIT
STAGE ENTRANCE
WHAT A NIGHT! CLEAR! REFRESHING!
LARRY DAVIS
SLUG 'IM!!
OOF!!!
1-18-49
FUNNYMAN—By Jerry Siegel and Joe Shuster
Louts Meet Loon
AFTER 'IM! DON'T LET HIM GET AWAY!
DON'T KNOW WHY THOSE THUGS JUMPED ME! AND I'M NOT WAITING TO FIND OUT!
BUT AS THE COMEDIAN ROUNDS A TURN IN THE ALLEY, HE SWIFTLY REVERSES IDENTITIES
IT WOULDN'T DO FOR PEOPLE TO REALIZE THAT LARRY DAVIS IS HANDY WITH HIS DUKES, AND SO...
...MEET FUNNYMAN!!!
??!
OH-OH! WE'RE IN FOR TROUBLE!

FUNNYMAN—By Jerry Siegel and Joe Shuster
Elusive Target
OUT OF OUR WAY, YOU PUTTY-NOSED PEST! WE DON'T WANT ANY TROUBLE WITH YOU!
BUT TROUBLE IS WHAT I'M GONNA GIVE YOU PLENTY OF!
YOU ASKED FOR IT!
TAKE THAT!
POW!
SOCK!
BRAVO, LADS! A SOCKO PERFORM-ANCE!
1-20-49
FUNNYMAN—By Jerry Siegel and Joe Shuster
Information Please
WHAT HIT ME?
I DID! AND YOU HIT ME WHEN FUNNYMAN DUCKED!
AWRIGHT! TALK! WHY DID YOU STRONG-ARMERS GANG-UP ON LARRY DAVIS?
MISS LEEDS ORDERED US TO BRING LARRY DAVIS TO A PARTY SHE'S TOSSING TONIGHT.
AND SHE TOLD US TO STOP AT NOTHING!
S'LONG, CHUMPS! TRY TO BEHAVE!
WHY, THAT--!!
FORGET THAT GOOF! MAYBE WE CAN STILL OVERTAKE LARRY DAVIS!

FUNNYMAN—By Jerry Siegel and Joe Shuster

Lovely to Look At

OUTDISTANCING LOLA LEEDS' HIRELINGS, FUNNYMAN TRANSFORMS HIMSELF BACK TO LARRY DAVIS, AND PERMITS HIMSELF TO BE OVERTAKEN.
COME ALONG PEACEABLY, AND YOU WON'T GET HURT.
ALL R-RIGHT. (I'LL LET 'EM TAKE ME IN TOW, JUST TO SEE WHAT GIVES.)
WHY BE UNHAPPY, DAVIS? WE'RE BRINGIN' YOU TO MISS LEEDS PARTY—AT HER REQUEST.
I'M PECULIAR, I GUESS. I LIKE TO GO TO PARTIES OF MY OWN FREE WILL.
BESIDES, WHY SHOULD I BE HAPPY TO MEET THE LEEDS GAL? LIKE MANY HEIRESSES, SHE'S PROBABLY BUCK-TOOTHED, SPINDLE-LEGGED, AND CROSS-EYED!
DAVIS... MEET MISS LOLA LEEDS!
GULP!
AND WHAT'S WRONG WITH YOU?
1-22-49

FUNNYMAN—By Jerry Siegel and Joe Shuster

Frame-up

FUNNYMAN—By Jerry Siegel and Joe Shuster **Desperate Measures**

FUNNYMAN—By Jerry Siegel and Joe Shuster **The Pay-off**

FUNNYMAN—By Jerry Siegel and Joe Shuster
Counterattack
TOP THAT, IF YOU CAN!
ORDERS ARE ORDERS!
SMACK
TRY RINGING THAT ONE UP ON YOUR CASH REGISTER, "BILLION-DOLLAR-BABY"!
(THE JACKPOT! ...WHAT A MAN!!!)
1-27-49
FUNNYMAN—By Jerry Siegel and Joe Shuster
It's a Gift
WHERE DID YOU DISAPPEAR TO?
LOLA LEEDS HAD SOME STRONG-ARM LADS TACKLE ME --THEN TRIED DAZZLING ME WITH HER ZILLIONS. SHE GOT NOWHERES.
NEXT MORNING.
IT MUST TICKLE YOUR EGO TO HAVE A RICH GAL LIKE LOLA GO GA-GA OVER YOU!
SHE PROBABLY HAS ALREADY FORGOTTEN THAT I EXIST.
WASSAT??!
I REPEAT--THIS CAR IS A GIFT TO YOU FROM MISS LEEDS. SORT OF A PEACE GESTURE!

FUNNYMAN—By Jerry Siegel and Joe Shuster **Taking Ways**

FUNNYMAN—By Jerry Siegel and Joe Shuster **His Lucky Day**

FUNNYMAN—By Jerry Siegel and Joe Shuster
Lady with Connections
REALLY, MISS LEEDS. YOU SHOULD BE MORE DISCREET.
AND WHAT HAVE I DONE NOW, FLEMINGWAY?
ACCORDING TO THE GOSSIP COLUMNS THIS MORNING YOU "MADE A PLAY FOR LARRY DAVIS, WERE SQUELCHED, AND NOW THE WHOLE TOWN'S LAUGHING."
I PAY YOU TO RUN MY BUSINESS, NOT MY HEART AFFAIRS. ... ONE OF MY ENTER-PRISES INCLUDES BEING MAJORITY STOCKHOLDER OF N.G. PICTURES MOVIE STUDIO. WHO RUNS IT?
SAM HILL.— WHY DO YOU ASK?
OPERATOR? --GET ME HOLLYWOOD!
2-1-49
FUNNYMAN—By Jerry Siegel and Joe Shuster
Change of Heart
THE PRIVATE ESTATE OF SAM HILL, EXECUTIVE PRODUCER OF N.G. PICTURES IN HOLLYWOOD.
IT'S FOR YOU, SIR. EMPIRE CITY CALLING!
I SHOULD BOTHER TO SPEAK TO EMPIRE CITY WHEN I CAN FLOAT IN MY $50,000 SWIMMING-POOL SURROUNDED BY STARLETS?
EMPIRE CITY CAN GO CHASE ITSELF!
BUT, MR. HILL, SIR! THE CALL IS FROM MISS LEEDS, THE STUDIO'S LARGEST STOCKHOLDER. AND SHE SAYS YOU'D BETTER ANSWER THE PHONE... OR ELSE!
MISS LEEDS!!... YOU FLAT-HEADED IDIOT! HOW DARE YOU DELAY AN URGENT PHONE CALL! YOU'RE FIRED!!
2-2-49

FUNNYMAN—By Jerry Siegel and Joe Shuster
Orders are Orders
IF THERE'S ANYTHING I CAN DO FOR YOU, MISS LEEDS... ANYTHING...!!!
YOU CAN HOP A PLANE AND REACH MY OFFICE BEFORE IT CLOSES... OR GET YOURSELF A NEW JOB!
LATER.
I'M SAM HILL. --WHAT IS IT THAT YOU WISH, MISS LEEDS?
I... WANT... LARRY... DAVIS!!!
A STUPENDOUS INSPIRATION! WE'LL MAKE LARRY DAVIS THE GREATEST COMEDIAN THE FILMS HAVE EVER KNOWN!
CORRECTION!-- TRAGEDIAN!!
2-3-49

FUNNYMAN—By Jerry Siegel and Joe Shuster
Lola's Inspiration
LARRY DAVIS... PLAY TRAGIC ROLES IN FILMS WE PRODUCE! YOU MUST BE JOKING!
THOSE ARE MY ORDERS!
YOURS IS NOT TO QUESTION WHY! DO AS I SAY, OR I'LL HIRE ANOTHER GLORIFIED OFFICE-BOY TO RUN N.G. PICTURES!
YOU-- (GULP!) WIN!
THIS IS DISASTROUS! MY LAST FEW PICTURES WERE FLOPS! IF THE DAVIS FILM IS A FAILURE ... AS IT'S BOUND TO BE... I'LL BE WASHED UP IN THE MOVIE GAME... THROUGH!!
2-4-49
I'VE GOT GREAT PLANS FOR LARRY! WHEN I FINISH WITH THE BOY, NO ONE WILL RECOGNIZE HIM!
LARRY DAVIS
THAT'S JUST WHAT WE'RE AFRAID OF!

FUNNYMAN—By Jerry Siegel and Joe Shuster
Surprise Meeting
YOW!... N.G. PICTURES HAS WIRED ME AN OFFER TO STAR IN MOVIES!
GREAT!
THAT'S ODD! YOU'RE ASKED TO PRESENT YOURSELF AT THEIR LOCAL BRANCH OFFICE WITHIN AN HOUR... ALONE!
HO! HO!-- LET'S NOT WORRY ABOUT PETTY DETAILS!
LATER.
N.G. PICTURES
MISS LEEDS! WH-WHAT ARE YOU DOING HERE?
I AM N.G. PICTURES!!
2-5-49
FUNNYMAN—By Jerry Siegel and Joe Shuster
Misunderstood Genius
SO YOU OWN N.G. PICTURES! THEN THAT TELEGRAPHED MOVIE OFFER WAS JUST ANOTHER GAG OF THE IRRESPONSIBLE LOLA LEEDS.
IT WAS ON THE LEVEL—AND HERE'S THE CONTRACT TO PROVE IT.
WHEWWW!-- I THOUGHT FIGURES LIKE THESE WERE ONLY USED TO MEASURE DISTANCES BETWEEN PLANETS! BUT HOW COME JUNE, HAPPY, AND THE REST OF MY TROUPE AREN'T MENTIONED?
WE'RE NOT INTERESTED IN SECOND RATERS. IT'S YOU WE WANT!
WELL, I DON'T KNOW. IF THE OTHERS ARE LEFT OUT IN THE COLD, THEN...
YOU FOOL! YOU'VE PERMITTED THOSE LEECHES TO SIDETRACK YOUR TRUE TALENTS TOO LONG!
FOR YEARS YOU'VE BEEN WASTING YOURSELF ON LOW-BROW TOMFOOLERY WHEN WITHIN YOU IS THE MAKINGS OF A GREAT DRAMATIC STAR!
ME?
2-7-49

FUNNYMAN—By Jerry Siegel and Joe Shuster

Convinced

FUNNYMAN—By Jerry Siegel and Joe Shuster

Sealed With A Kiss

FUNNYMAN—By Jerry Siegel and Joe Shuster
Poor Little Rich Girl
ENROUTE TO HOLLYWOOD.
YOU'RE A STRANGE GIRL, LOLA. ONE MINUTE HARD AS NAILS... THE NEXT SECOND, SWEET AND...
DESIRABLE?
I'M NOT REALLY HARD, LARRY. BUT IT'S DIFFICULT NOT TO BE CYNICAL, ESPECIALLY WHEN PEOPLE MAKE LITTLE SECRET OF IT THAT THEY'RE PRIMARILY ATTRACTED TO YOUR BANKROLL.
ALL MY LIFE I'VE DREAMED OF MEETING SOMEONE KIND AND UNDERSTANDING, AND SINCERE... SOMEONE I COULD REALLY CARE FOR...
I HOPE YOU MEET THAT SOMEONE... SOON.
I BELIEVE I HAVE!
FUNNYMAN—By Jerry Siegel and Joe Shuster
Reception Committee
HOLLYWOOD!
YOU MUST BE MY HOUSE-GUEST DURING YOUR STAY!
THANKS, HILL!
I'LL CALL FOR YOU TONIGHT, LARRY. WE'LL DO THE TOWN. YOU CAN REPORT TO WORK AT THE STUDIO IN THE MORNING.
MAKE YOURSELF AT HOME! I DON'T WANT YOU TO EVER FORGET YOUR VISIT HERE!
I'M SURE I WON'T.
THAT NIGHT.
YOU GENTLEMEN WILL SEE TO IT THAT DAVIS NEVER FORGETS HIS VISIT HERE, RIGHT?
RIGHT!

FUNNYMAN—By Jerry Siegel and Joe Shuster
Frightening Prospect
I RAISED YOU THREE ACTORS TO HORROR FILM STARDOM... AND NOW AS MONSTER-BOY, THE HUMAN FOX, AND THE GREEN GHOST... YOU CAN REPAY THE FAVOR...
... BY TERRIFYING LARRY DAVIS SO MUCH HE'LL SKEEDADDLE OUT OF TOWN. I CAN'T LET HIM PLAY A TRAGIC ROLE IN FILMS OR HE'LL FLOP. AFTER MY RECENT FAILURES, IT WOULD RUIN ME!
HERE HE IS, NOW. YOU KNOW WHAT TO DO.
THE EVENING WAS FUN. MUST WE PART SO SOON?
GOTTA REPORT BRIGHT AND EARLY TO THE STUDIO YOU HAPPEN TO OWN--BOSS!
2-12-49

FUNNYMAN—By Jerry Siegel and Joe Shuster
Uninvited Caller
LARRY DAVIS IS ABOUT TO ENJOY HIS FIRST EVENING AS THE HOUSE-GUEST OF MOVIE PRODUCER SAM HILL.
HOORAY FOR HOLLYWOOD! WHO'D HAVE EVER THOUGHT AN UPSTART KID FROM TENTH AVENUE WOULD EVER WIND UP IN A SWANK DUMP LIKE THIS?
AND NOW TO CRAWL INTO MY COZY LITTLE OUTSIZE BED AND DREAM GREAT DREAMS OF FILM STARDOM!
2-14-49

FUNNYMAN—By Jerry Siegel and Joe Shuster **House of Chills**

FUNNYMAN—By Jerry Siegel and Joe Shuster **Chase Sequence**

FUNNYMAN—By Jerry Siegel and Joe Shuster **What a Knight**

FUNNYMAN—By Jerry Siegel and Joe Shuster **The Figure at the Door**

FUNNYMAN—By Jerry Siegel and Joe Shuster — **Unmasked**

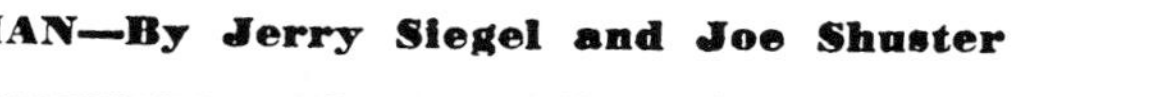

FUNNYMAN—By Jerry Siegel and Joe Shuster — **Passing of a Hero**

FUNNYMAN—By Jerry Siegel and Joe Shuster
Fly-By-Knight
HOORAY! WE'VE FINISHED OFF FUNNYMAN!
WE'LL BE FAMOUS!
FAMOUS-SCHMAMOUS! LET'S GET THE JOB OVER WITH!
(GULP!) L-LOOK!
BACK TO THE WATER'S SURFACE FLOATS A RIGID FIGURE . . .
IMPOSSIBLE! IT COULDN'T FLOAT!
YEE-EE! IT'S FLYING!
2-22-49
FUNNYMAN—By Jerry Siegel and Joe Shuster
Explanation
TH' GHOST O' FUNNYMAN IS FLYIN' AFTER US!!
EXPLANATION: FUNNYMAN HAD AGILELY FREED HIMSELF FROM THE SINKING ARMOR.
(REAR EXIT!)
(FIRST I PLACE A FUNNYMAN FACE-MASK IN THE EMPTY VISOR...!
2-23-49
NEXT, FUNNYMAN INFLATES A LARGE BALLOON WITHIN THE ARMOR WITH CHEMICALS THAT COMBINE TO FORM HELIUM!
(UP...AN' AT 'EM!)

FUNNYMAN—By Jerry Siegel and Joe Shuster
Downfall
TH' GHOST O' FUNNYMAN!
GHOST OR NOT, HERE'S WHERE I FIX HIM!
BANG!
BOSTON BLOOIE'S BULLET PENETRATES THE FUNNYMAN FACE-MASK, PUNCTURING THE HELIUM-INFLATED BALLOON.
SSS-SS
A DIRECT HIT!
KLUNK
YOWCH!
2-24-49
FUNNYMAN—By Jerry Siegel and Joe Shuster
Rogue's Retreat
HILL'S THREE HIRELINGS... THE GREEN GHOST, MONSTER BOY, AND THE HUMAN FOX... REVIVE...
ULP!
D-DID YOU SEE THAT?
I D-DID!
RUN! RUN FER YER LIVES!
WHAT WAS THAT??!
GIVE US ROOM! WE'RE SCRAMMING, TOO!!
2-25-49
HO! HO!—AND NOW THAT I'VE TROUNCED THOSE BAD BOYS, IT'S TIME TO CHANGE BACK TO LARRY DAVIS AND CARRY ON!!

FUNNYMAN—By Jerry Siegel and Joe Shuster
Larry Davis Slept Here
(CHUCKLE!) AFTER THE RECEPTION MY HORROR-ACTORS GAVE LARRY DAVIS, HE IS PROBABLY HALF-WAY BACK TO EMPIRE CITY BY NOW!
??? (HE'S HERE! ...SOUND ASLEEP!) ???
2-26-49
AFTER HILL STAGGERS OFF.
WHETHER SAM HILL LIKES IT OR NOT, THE SHOW WILL GO ON! ...JUST THINK! TOMORROW I PLAY GREAT LOVER BEFORE THE CAMERAS...AND FOR MONEY, YET!

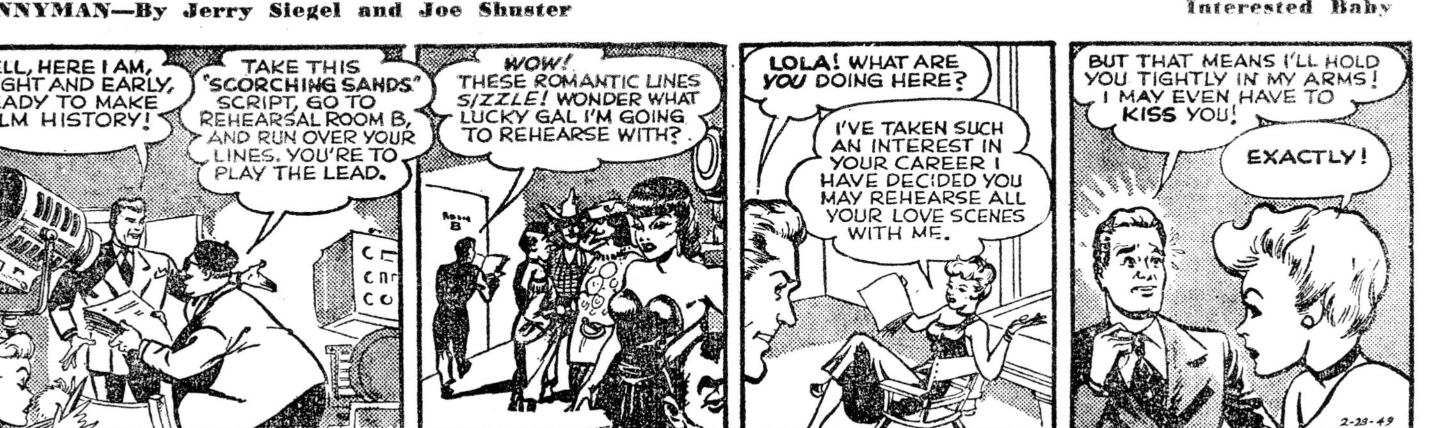
FUNNYMAN—By Jerry Siegel and Joe Shuster
Interested Baby
WELL, HERE I AM, BRIGHT AND EARLY, READY TO MAKE FILM HISTORY!
TAKE THIS "SCORCHING SANDS" SCRIPT, GO TO REHEARSAL ROOM B, AND RUN OVER YOUR LINES. YOU'RE TO PLAY THE LEAD.
WOW! THESE ROMANTIC LINES SIZZLE! WONDER WHAT LUCKY GAL I'M GOING TO REHEARSE WITH?
ROOM B
LOLA! WHAT ARE YOU DOING HERE?
I'VE TAKEN SUCH AN INTEREST IN YOUR CAREER I HAVE DECIDED YOU MAY REHEARSE ALL YOUR LOVE SCENES WITH ME.
BUT THAT MEANS I'LL HOLD YOU TIGHTLY IN MY ARMS! I MAY EVEN HAVE TO KISS YOU!
EXACTLY!
2-28-49

FUNNYMAN—By Jerry Siegel and Joe Shuster
"A Smacking Success"
"BABUSHKA, MY DARLING! I THIRST FOR YOUR LIPS."
"DRINK!"
NO! NO! THAT AWKWARD PECK WOULD NEVER DO. YOU'RE TO PLAY THE ROLE OF A MAD LOVER, NOT A WAX DUMMY!
AND I SUPPOSE YOU COULD DO BETTER?
ULP! YOU CAN!!!
3-1-49
FUNNYMAN—By Jerry Siegel and Joe Shuster
"Interruption"
RUN OVER THOSE LINES AGAIN. THIS TIME, LET'S HAVE A LITTLE ROMANTIC FIRE!
H-RRUF!-- THE EMBERS ARE STIRRING ALREADY!
"DARLING! DEAREST! BELOVED! WHEN YOU'RE NEAR ME LIKE THIS, MY HEART BEATS LIKE A FRENZIED JUNGLE TOM-TOM!"
3-2-49
HAW! HAW!
VERY FUNNY!
J-JUNE! "HAPPY"! AND "THE GANG"!

"Say It Isn't So!"

FUNNYMAN—By Jerry Siegel and Joe Shuster

"Parting"

FUNNYMAN—By Jerry Siegel and Joe Shuster
Swell Guy
I FEEL LIKE A HEEL, TURNING ON MY FRIENDS, QUITTING THE TROUPE. MAYBE I'VE MADE A MISTAKE.
NO! YOU'LL NEVER REGRET YOUR DECISION!
HERE'S TO THE NEW LARRY DAVIS! HERE'S TO THE COUNTRY'S NEWEST AND GREATEST SCREEN IDOL!
YEAH. HERE'S TO A SWELL GUY!
MEANWHILE, ON SOUND STAGE "E"...
AFTER ALL OUR YEARS IN BETTER-GRADE FILMS, APPEARING WITH A SLAPSTICK MORON LIKE LARRY DAVIS IS REVOLTING!
OUR REPUTATIONS WILL SUFFER!
THE NERVE OF THE UPSTART! SWITCHING TO DRAMA, FROM LOW COMEDY!
2-8-49
I DON'T WANT HIM IN THE FILM ANY MORE THAN YOU DO. I'VE A PLAN HOW WE CAN MAKE HIM LOOK SO RIDICULOUS, HE'LL QUIT IN ANGER.
TELL US MORE!
FUNNYMAN—By Jerry Siegel and Joe Shuster
Anti-social Splash
YOUR FIRST ASSIGNMENT IS SIMPLE. JUST STAND RIGHT THERE, AND LOOK TOUGH.
THAT SHOULDN'T BE TOUGH. HA! HA!
THAT, I PRESUME, IS HUMOR!
YOU KNOW WHAT TO DO!
RIGHT!
SPLASH!
FOOL! I OUGHT TO FIRE YOU!
(FIRED? I'LL GET A BONUS!)
3-7-49
FORGET IT. IT WAS JUST AN ACCIDENT.

FUNNYMAN—By Jerry Siegel and Joe Shuster **Pie From the Sky**

FUNNYMAN—By Jerry Siegel and Joe Shuster **It's No Joke**

FUNNYMAN—By Jerry Siegel and Joe Shuster

Larry Catches On

FUNNYMAN—By Jerry Siegel and Joe Shuster

Sprinkle, Sprinkle, Little Star

FUNNYMAN—By Jerry Siegel and Joe Shuster

Gone With the Wind

FUNNYMAN—By Jerry Siegel and Joe Shuster

An Earful

FUNNYMAN—By Jerry Siegel and Joe Shuster **Next Victim**

FUNNYMAN—By Jerry Siegel and Joe Shuster **Dismissed**

FUNNYMAN—By Jerry Siegel and Joe Shuster
Free at Last
I DON'T WANT YOU CLUTTERING UP THIS STUDIO. GET OUT!!
(CHOKE!)
YIPPEE! I'M RID OF LOLA AND THAT CONTRACT!
3-17-49
BUT WAIT! JUNE AND THE GANG ARE HEADED BACK FOR EMPIRE CITY CONVINCED I'M A LOUSE. GOTTA REMEDY THAT!
FUNNYMAN—By Jerry Siegel and Joe Shuster
Casual Visitor
A PARACHUTING FIGURE TUMBLES OUT OF A CHARTERED PLANE.
STOP THE BUS!!!
OKAY, LADY.
3-18-49
LARRY! WHAT ARE YOU DOING HERE?
JUST THOUGHT I'D DROP IN!

FUNNYMAN—By Jerry Siegel and Joe Shuster

Together Again

October 18, 1948 to October 26, 1948. "Origin Story."
Competitors are zooming past comedian Larry Davis in the popularity polls. Thus, his manager June Farrell decides to try a publicity stunt to attract public attention: Larry dons a clown suit and pretends to be a crime fighter named Funnyman who uses "pokes and jokes" to defeat criminals. However, he fights real criminals by mistake and likes it so much that he decides to continue his Funnyman identity even though June is worried that he might get hurt.

October 27, 1948 to November 27, 1948. "The Jet-Jalopy Caper"
In a sensuous, low-cut dress, June awaits Larry's arrival for a date but is surprised when Funnyman shows up instead. The clown whistles for his car and it arrives at their window ten stories up. June goes for a ride she will "never forget" in his Jet-Jalopy. Funnyman stashes his car behind some bushes to change back to Larry Davis in order to take June nightclubbing. But, Harold Stone, a near-sighted crook, finds the fabulous jalopy and pilfers it. Stone has been a pitiful failure as a crook but he uses the car to commit a series of daring robberies. He engages in a duel in the Jet-Jalopy with Funnyman riding his Trix-cycle. Funnyman has outfitted the cycle with gimmicks which fend off Stone's attacks: A net protects Funnyman so that when Stone drops a cement block on the cycle it boomerangs back and hits his car. Then Funnyman radio waves a signal to the jalopy and it hits Stone in the face with a pie and squirts him with lemonade, then his car seat propels him onto the pavement below where he is captured by Funnyman and the police.

The first Funnyman strip, October 18, 1948.

October 29, 1948 to December 18, 1948. "Funnyman vs. Bighead."

In this tale, Siegel recycles his first superman from his 1933 science fiction fanzine about a telepathic genius who could control minds. Funnyman battles Bighead, a bald, big-domed criminal who invents a "Mental Miracle Machine" which allows him to control objects and people though his commands. Bighead uses his powers to commit a number of miraculous crimes, like causing streams of money to flow out of teller's cages at a bank. A comic battle ensues with Bighead causing Funnyman's body to lengthen and expand like a balloon, as if it were a reflection in a funhouse hall of mirrors, then shrink to the size of a mouse. Funnyman is able to defeat him by tricking him into wishing he had never been born and, due to his Mental Miracle Machine, his wish comes true.

December 20, 1948 to January 12, 1949. "Crime Doesn't Pay."

Joe Dope, a dimwitted, two-bit hood, wants to become a big-shot gangster. Thinking it will make him famous, Joe tries to get Funnyman to arrest him, but the clown resists attempts. To teach Joe a lesson, Funnyman disguises himself as Bumphrey Hogart, a Humphrey Bogart clone, and enlists Joe as his helper. Funnyman pretends to order his gang to kill Joe because he might squeal on them then fakes a ferocious battle with the gang offstage. When Funnyman emerges ready to take Joe on too, the petty thief tells the clown he has reformed and begs the clown to let him go. Ironically after he decides to go straight he is finally arrested—for jaywalking.

January 13, 1949 to March 19, 1949. "Adventure in Hollywood."

The spoiled and tyrannical Lola Leeds is the richest woman in the world. She falls for Larry and when he rejects her overture she orders her hoods to bring him to her by force. When he agrees to go along peaceably to see what's up, she has Larry entertain her guests but imperiously tells him she won't pay him unless he's funny. She has secretly told no one to laugh, wanting to break his spirit and humble him. Larry responds with a joke of his own—a hand-buzzer. When she slaps him he puts her in her place with a sizzling kiss that leaves her declaring, "What a man!"

FUNNYMAN—By Jerry Siegel and Joe Shuster — What Every Girl Shouldn't Know

A sensuous shot of June waiting for her boyfriend Larry Davis a.k.a. Funnyman, October 27, 1948.

Larry refuses to be bought by her luxurious presents so she decides to offer him a contract at a movie studio that she owns. She exerts her control by trying to make the comedian into a serious dramatic actor. Dazzled by her beauty and the chance to be a movie star, Larry deserts June and his friends. Lola orders director Sam Hill to make a tragedy starring Larry but Hill tries to sabotage Larry because he thinks the movie will be a failure and, with a string of flops behind him, will ruin him in Hollywood. He orders three horror film stars—Monster Boy, The Human Fox, and The Green Ghost—to scare Larry away. But Funnyman dons a suit of armor and scares them away instead—with the help of a hidden balloon which makes him appear to fly—à la Superman. Larry finally learns his lesson when Lola two-times him, and she breaks his contract freeing him to return to Empire City where June and the gang accept his apologies.

March 21, 1949 to April 28, 1949. "Numbskull."

Funnyman battles Numbskull, "the most terrifying bully in the city's toughest slum district." Numbskull goes on a rage if any man even talks to Peaches, his moll. In order to bring the tough guy down, Funnyman has a "date" with Peaches, which devolves into a knockdown fight with the tough.

April 29, 1949 to June 1, 1949. "Reforming Chip."

A gang of juvenile delinquents attacks Funnyman during a robbery and the police capture one of them named Chip Willis. Larry agrees to take Chip into his custody and tries to reform him. His efforts succeed until Chip leaves because he doesn't want to be Larry's prisoner. Chip's gang hold Larry prisoner until Chip helps him escape. Funnyman enlists Chip's aid to fight the gang in costume as Funnyboy, à la Batman and Robin. Then, Larry places Chip in a military school where he gets the discipline he needs.

Bighead makes Funnyman's body expand and contract as if in a funhouse mirror, December 13, 1948.

June 2, 1949 to July 1, 1949. "The Man Who Returned."
Funnyman stops a man from committing suicide. Thought dead, Frank Conway, the famous industrialist, has developed amnesia. The last thing he remembers is being told by his general manager, Jack Prentice, that his accountant, Jim Taylor, has embezzled $250,000 from the company and confronting Taylor with his crime. Frank was found unconscious and is taken in by a farmer and his daughter, Amy. Amy falls in love with him but for some reason Frank holds back. He recovers his memory after being hit by a bull, saving Amy from its charge, and remembers that he has a wife and son. Frank discovers that Prentice, his most trusted friend, has been courting his wife in his absence. Frank attempted suicide because he thought his family would be happier without him. With the aid of Funnyman, Frank discovers that Prentice was stealing more money from the company than Taylor, and that Prentice caused his amnesia by hitting him on the head before he could phone the police. The thieves dumped the body in the river, and Taylor blackmailed Prentice, claiming that he had killed Frank. Frank and Funnyman rout the crooks, and Frank reunites with his family.

July 2, 1949 to July 29, 1949. "The Winston Wildcat."
Although the strip retains the Funnyman title it now stars a new character, the rich youth Reggie Van Twerp who is menaced by a number of schemers, usually women out to get his fortune. In this story, his domineering Aunt Lucy makes him propose to Clarice Winston, a seemingly quiet, "old-fashioned girl." But Clarice turns out to be a hellion who creates a near-riot at a dance club when she throws a pie in the face of a boring speaker, then has a high-speed chase with the police and angered hotel workers, crashing her car. When they return to Reggie's mansion, Reggie has to climb a curtain to escape her sexual advances. She dumps a bowl of water on Aunt Lucy's head when Lucy blames Reggie for luring the innocent girl into his den and reveals that she is not really Clarice but her sister Janice, "The Winston Wildcat."

July 30, 1949 to August 19, 1949. "The Marriage Trap."

Reggie hires a male secretary named Higgins who gets him out of near-scrapes with different schemers. In this story Goldie and her mother claim that Reggie has invited them for the weekend as houseguests. Though Reggie can't remember the invitation he goes along with it thinking he has just forgotten the matter. Goldie turns out to be a gold digger, and she tries to force Reggie into marrying her by pretending to faint, then tries to lure Reggie into stealing a kiss while she is unconscious. Higgins foils the plot by dousing her backside with ice cubes, then forcing Goldie and her mother to leave by telling them that Reggie is a Jekyll-and-Hyde creature who turns into a beast at ten o'clock.

August 20, 1949 to August 26, 1949. "Slumming for Scholarship."

Determined to prove that he is not a rich ne'er-do-well, Reggie wants to penetrate the underworld so that he can write a scholarly tome about it. Reggie is set up to be robbed by Lil, another blonde femme fatale, until saved by Higgins.

August 27. 1949 to c. September 17, 1949. "The Super-Brain."

Professor Fizz promises to create a serum which will make Reggie into a "super-brain," so that he will let Fizz and his gold-bricking relatives move into his mansion. The relatives create havoc and insult the youth's snobby guests until Higgins finds a way to get them and Fuzz to leave.

About the Authors

Mel Gordon is Professor of Theatre Arts at the University of California, Berkeley and the author of over 130 articles on American, French, German, Israeli, Italian, Russian, and Yiddish theatre. His books include *Dada Performance*; *Erik Jan Hanussen: Hitler's Jewish Clairvoyant*; *Expressionist Texts*; *The Grand Guignol: The Theatre of Horror and Terror*; *Harold Clurman: A Life in the Theatre*; *Lazzi: the Comic Routines of the Commedia dell'arte*; *Meyerhold, Eisenstein, and Biomechanics: Revolutionary Acting in Soviet Russia* [co-authored with Alma Law]; *Mikhoels the Wise*; *The Seven Addictions and Five Professions of Anita Berber*; *Stanislavsky in America: An Actor's Workbook*; and *Voluptuous Panic: the Erotic World of Weimar Berlin*.

Thomas Andrae (Ph.D. University of California, Berkeley) is an internationally recognized authority on social theory and popular culture. He is an instructor in Sociology at California State University East Bay, and co-founder and senior editor of *Discourse: Journal for Theoretical Studies in Media and Culture*. His work has been reprinted in *American Media and Mass Culture* (University of California Press, 1987), and *A Comics Studies Reader* (University Press of Mississippi, 2008). He is the author of seven books on comics, popular culture, social theory, and American history, including *Carl Barks and the Disney Comic Book: Unmasking the Myth of Modernity*, *Creators of the Superheroes*, and *TV Nation: Prime Time Television and the Politics of the Sixties*, and co-author of Bob Kane's autobiography, *Batman & Me*. Mr. Andrae has produced a documentary about comics legend Carl Barks and is featured in the Warner Bros. *The Bob Kane Story*, among other documentaries.

Danny Fingeroth was a longtime editor and writer at Marvel Comics. He is the author of *Disguised as Clark Kent: Jews, Comics, and the Creation of the Superhero* and *Superman on the Couch: What Superheroes Really Tell Us About Ourselves and Our Society* (both from Continuum). Fingeroth has spoken at The Smithsonian Institution and The Metropolitan Museum of Art. He is currently senior vice president of Education at New York's Museum of Comic and Cartoon Art (MoCCA), and on the board of directors of The Institute for Comics Studies.

www.FeralHouse.com